Dr. Tesla F. Johnson has, in a wonderful way, presented to us the events as recorded in scripture, of God's plan for His creation. I believe you will find this to be a marvelous study to guide you to a greater understanding of the past and the future journey of man-kind, as contained in God's Holy Word.

The highlight for me was the charts that documented the sequence of events from the beginning of creation. The Lord will bless you as you read and study this book.

—**Rev. Bob Walker**
Pastor, Bay Street Baptist Church

What an incredible journey through the events recorded in the Word of God! Dr. Tesla F. Johnson, Frank to me, has with exquisite detail taken us through, step by step, the undeniable and miraculous events which bring us to where we are in our world today. Throughout the book Frank beautifully weaves the message of salvation as he takes us through biblical history. I believe "From Eternity to Eternity" can be a powerful resource for believers, as well as seekers. Frank has shared his overwhelming knowledge of the Word on every page, and he has shared his heart for all those who do not know Jesus Christ as their personal Lord and Savior.

What a blessing!

—**Donna Perman-Welsh**
Bay Street Baptist Church

May our God richly bless and keep you according to His riches in glory.
Tesla F. Johnson
Jeremiah 29:11

From Eternity to Eternity

From Eternity to Eternity

The Events of History as Indicated in Scripture

Tesla F. Johnson Ph.D.

WinePress Publishing (PO Box 428, Enumclaw, WA 98022) functions only as book publisher. As such, the ultimate design, content, editorial accuracy, and views expressed or implied in this work are those of the author.

ISBN 13: 978-1-4141-2382-0
ISBN 10: 1-4141-2382-5
Library of Congress Catalog Card Number: 2010927352

For my Savior and Lord, Jesus Christ,
who has the power to save all who trust in
Him as their Savior from an eternity in hell

Contents

Acknowledgments

I would like to thank all the wonderful people who God has allowed to come into my life to help me become more like what He wants me to be.

Thank you to all of the people who had a part in making this book a reality. A special thanks goes to Reverend Frank Scott, Reverend Jim DuBois, Reverend Mark Douglas, Dr. Diane H. Cross, Doris Barrell, Joan Earll, Reverend Don Miller, Hugh A. Davis, Robb and Virginia Scuderi, Robert and Julie Houtz, Carol Lanier, Reverend Bob Walker, Donna Perman-Welsh, Minister of Music and Senior Adults, and all those people behind the scenes who reviewed this book and had a part in bringing it to publication.

A special thanks goes to my dear wife, Eleanor R. Johnson; my father, Dr. T. Farris Johnson; and my mother, Ruby S. Johnson—all of whom have been called home by God.

Again, thank you to each person and to the one and only true and living God for all the assistance in making this book a reality.

PREFACE

For years I struggled to understand in what order the major events of the Bible occurred. For example, in Revelation 12:3–4, John tells of Satan causing one-third of the angels to join him in a rebellion against God. When did this occur? Revelation is the last book of the Bible. Does that mean this had already occurred? If so, when did it occur? Or is it to occur sometime in the future? Even though I had studied the Bible for many years, I still had many questions about these and many other verses. I am a very analytical person, so the events must be in order for them to make sense to me.

I believe God's Word contains the answers to these questions and to many more besides. In this book, I examine various passages of Scripture to determine which major events have already taken place, which ones are happening now, and which ones are yet to come. I also discuss what will happen at the end of time and whether or not all people will go through the same events. In this way, I hope to give the reader a well-rounded appreciation of the past, present, and future events of the Bible.

—**Tesla F. Johnson,** Ph.D.

CHAPTER 1

PROOF THAT THE BIBLE IS TRUE

Some people do not believe in God's existence at all. Others are unsure but have serious doubts as to whether there could be a God who controls the events in people's lives. Still others know and believe in their hearts that God exists and that He is very real. These individuals believe this same God wants to walk and talk with them. From this, we see that when it comes to belief in God, there are two extremes: (1) those who believe there is no God, and (2) those who believe there is a true and living God.

Which is the better position to take? Let's assume that a person who believes there is a true and living God dies and finds out there is no God at all. This person will not have lost anything at all, because he or she will have lived a good life according to the principles outlined in the Bible. However, if a person who does not believe in God dies and finds out there is, in fact, a true and living God, that person will have lost everything. Because that person did not believe in the one and only true, living God and trust in Him for salvation, he or she will spend eternity in hell.

The claims made in this book about which events have occurred in the past, which are occurring now, and which will occur in the future are based on the Bible. Of course, for those who do not believe in God's existence and do not accept the authority of Scripture, these arguments will not be compelling. While Paul says in 2 Timothy 3:16 that "all Scripture is given by inspiration of God, and is profitable for doctrine, for reproof, for correction, for instruction in righteousness," many people require more concrete proof. For this reason, three proofs will be presented in this chapter to show that the Bible is true, that it is the Word of God, and that its writing must have been directed by a supreme being.

Proof #1: How the Bible Was Written

The Bible was written over a period of about sixteen-hundred years, from approximately 1445 B.C. to A.D. 100, by forty different authors. Many of the authors were not aware of the others' writings or even the others had ever existed. The writers were people with varying backgrounds and occupations and included kings, statesmen, priests, learned men, herdsmen, tax collectors, fishermen, and physicians. As mentioned before, a gap of approximately sixteen hundred years separated the first author from the last.

Despite the fact the Bible was written by a number of different authors and the authors had varied backgrounds, when the Bible was assembled, it was consistent in its entirety, with no errors. For all intents and purposes, the odds of this occurring without guidance from a supreme being are about zero. It would be impossible.

Think of it this way: Imagine there are forty different people who are each making a part of a watch. These workmen have never seen a blueprint or a plan for the watch. Some of these workmen have never seen the other workers or don't know about the parts the others have made. These workmen labored over a sixteen-hundred-year period, until the final worker assembled the watch. Then, when the watch was wound up, it ran perfectly and kept perfect time. If this occurred, one would have to conclude that it was a miracle and that some supreme being had been in charge of those workers who had made the watch.

So, it is with the Bible. A supreme being called *God* was in charge of all those people who wrote it. Therefore, the Bible is God's Word.

Proof #2: Fulfilled Prophecies in the Bible

"Probability" is the chance that something will happen or will not happen. For example, if you take five black balls and four white balls and place them in an opaque jar, the chance that you will reach into the jar and get one black ball is five (the number of black balls in the jar) divided by nine (the total number of balls in the jar). This means that the chance of getting one black ball in one draw is 5/9. Likewise, if you place nine black balls in the opaque jar with no white balls, the probability that you will select a white ball is zero. It will not happen, because there are no white balls in the jar. On the other hand, the probability that you will select a black ball is one, meaning that it *will* happen because there are only black balls in the jar. In other words, probability is a number between zero and one. When the probability is zero, the event cannot happen; when the probability is one, the event will definitely happen.

Let's apply these laws of probability to the Bible, especially as they relate to the prophecies fulfilled in Scripture. When we examine the prophecies in the Old Testament that were fulfilled by the coming of Christ, we find that the number reaches more than three hundred. In an attempt to determine the statistical probability of one man fulfilling all of these major prophecies concerning the Messiah, one California mathematician, Peter Stoner (1888–1980), conducted an experiment with one of his classes. He assigned each student a messianic prophecy to study, with the goal of determining the statistical chance that the event could have been predicted without supernatural inspiration. For example, concerning the prophecy in Micah 5:2, which says the Messiah would be born in Bethlehem, Stoner and his students determined the average population from the time of Micah to the present and then divided this number by the average population of the earth during the same period. They concluded that the probability of one man being born in Bethlehem was one in 300,000.

After examining eight different prophecies, they conservatively estimated that the probability of one man fulfilling all eight was one in 10^{17} (10 followed by 17 zeros). In this way, Professor Stoner determined that the probability that one man could simultaneously fulfill each of the forty-eight messianic prophecies was one in 10^{181} (10 followed by 181 zeros).[1] Such a phenomenon as this is found in no other book in the world. The scientific conclusion is that the Bible must have had a supreme being, called *God,* who guided its construction and writing and fulfilled its prophecies in order for it to be as it is: *true* and God's Word.

Proof #3: How the Bible Survived

Over the centuries, enemies of the Bible have attacked it and attempted to physically destroy it. From the time of the Roman emperors to the more recent Communist regimes, many have tried to burn it, ban it, and outlaw it.[2] Yet the Bible has survived all of these attacks and today is the number one bestseller of all time. It has survived time, persecution, and criticism. As Josh McDowell notes, "Being written on material that perishes, having to be copied and recopied for hundreds of years before the invention of the printing press, did not diminish its style, correctness or existence. The Bible, compared with other ancient writings, has more manuscript evidence than any 10 pieces of classical literature combined."[3]

John Warwick Montgomery says that "to be skeptical of the resultant text of the New Testament books is to allow all of classical antiquity to slip into obscurity, for no documents of the ancient period are as well attested bibliographically as the New Testament."[4]

Bernard Ramm adds the following about the accuracy of the Bible and the number of biblical manuscripts in existence:

> Jews preserved it as no other manuscript has ever been preserved. With their massora (parva, magna, and finalis) they kept tabs on every letter, syllable, word, and paragraph. They had special classes of men within their culture whose sole duty was to preserve and transmit these documents with practically perfect fidelity—scribes, lawyers, massoretes. Who ever counted the letters and syllables and words of Plato or Aristotle? Cicero or Seneca?[5]

In *The Greatest Book in the World*, John Lea notes that a writer for the *North American Review* once made some interesting comparisons between the writings of William Shakespeare and the Bible. The article showed that much greater care had been taken in preserving the accuracy of the biblical texts than other writings, including Shakespeare's, even when there were more opportunities to preserve the more modern texts because of printed copies (versus printing by hand). Lea states:

> It seems strange that the text of Shakespeare, which has been in existence less than two hundred and eight years, should be far more uncertain and corrupt than that of the New Testament, now over eighteen centuries old, during nearly fifteen (centuries) of which it existed only in manuscript.... With perhaps a dozen or twenty exceptions, the text of every verse in the New Testament can be said to be so far settled by general consent of scholars, that any dispute as to its readings must relate rather to the interpretation of the words than to any doubts respecting the words themselves. But in every one of Shakespeare's thirty-seven plays there are probably a hundred readings still in dispute, a large portion of which materially affect the meaning of the passages in which they occur.[6]

The fact that the Bible has survived into modern times is, in fact, a miracle in itself. In A.D. 303, the Roman emperor Diocletian issued an edict in an attempt to stop the spread of Christianity. The imperial letter ordered churches to be razed and all Scripture to be destroyed by fire, warning that those who held high positions in society would lose all of their civil rights and those in their households would be deprived of their liberty if they persisted to profess Christ as Lord.[7] The irony is that a mere twenty-five years later, the emperor Constantine, Diocletian's successor, issued another edict, stating that fifty copies of the Scriptures should be prepared at the expense of the government.[8] Such a reversal indicates that there must have been a divine plan in ensuring that the Bible would survive throughout the generations.

The Bible has also withstood the attacks of skeptics who, over the centuries, have doubted its truths and attempted to malign it. Voltaire, the noted French Enlightenment philosopher and author, once stated that in one hundred years from his time Christianity would be swept from existence and pass into history. Instead, it is Voltaire who has passed into history, while the Bible has continued to increase and now can be found in almost every region in the world, blessing all those it touches. As Sidney Collett states in *All About the Bible*, "The English Cathedral in Zanzibar is built on the site of the Old Slave Market, and the Communion Table stands on the very spot where the whipping-post once stood! The world abounds with such instances.... As one has truly said, 'we might as well put our shoulder to the burning wheel of the sun, and try to stop it on its flaming course, as attempt to stop the circulation of the Bible.'"[9]

John W. Lea adds:

> Infidels for 1800 years have been refuting and overthrowing this book [the Bible], and yet it stands today as solid as a rock. Its circulation increases, and it is loved, cherished and read today more than ever before. Infidels, with all their assaults, make about as much impression on this book as a man with a tack hammer would on the Pyramids of Egypt. When the French monarch proposed the persecution of the Christians in his dominion, an old statesman and warrior said to him, "Sire, the Church of God is an anvil that has worn out many hammers." So the hammers of infidels have been pecking away at this book for ages, but the hammers are worn out, and the anvil still endures. If the Bible had not been the book of God, men would have destroyed it long ago. Emperors and popes, kings, priest, princes, and rulers have all tried their hand at it; they died and the book still lives.[10]

Many of the attacks against the Bible's authorship are also falling by the wayside. One such theory is called *The Documentary Hypothesis*. This hypothesis states that the Pentateuch (the first five books of the Bible) was originally derived from independent, parallel narratives and then combined into one document by a series of redactors, or editors. One of the reasons this theory gained prominence, aside from the different names used for God in the book of Genesis, was the belief the Hebrew language simply could not have evolved by the time the Pentateuch was supposed to have been written down by Moses. The logical conclusion, based on this reasoning, was that later authors had constructed all of the writings and stories in the Pentateuch.[11]

But then archeologists uncovered the "black stele." This ancient artifact was seven-and-a-half inches high and made of black diorite rock. The top of the stele depicted the Mesopotamian god Shamash giving laws to King Hammurabi (these eventually became known as the Code of Hammurabi). What is interesting is that this stele contained a definite writing system, yet it *predated* Moses' writings by at least three centuries! This proved that there was a system of writing in place at the time of Moses.[12]

Josh McDowell notes:

> What an irony of history! The "Documentary Hypothesis" is still taught, yet much of its original basis ("the assured results of higher criticism") has been eradicated and shown to be false. The "assured results of higher criticism" said there were no Hittites at the time of Abraham, for there were no other records of them apart from the Old Testament. They must be a myth. Well, wrong again. As the results of archaeology, there are now hundreds of references overlapping more than 1,200 years of Hittite civilization.[13]

Nelson Glueck (1900–1971), former president of the Jewish Theological Seminary in the Hebrew Union College in Cincinnati and one of the pioneers in biblical archeology, once said, "I've been accused of teaching the verbal, plenary inspiration of the Scripture. I want it to be understood that I have never taught this. All I have ever said is that in all of my archaeological investigation I have never found one artifact of antiquity that contradicts any statement of the Word of God."[14]

Robert Dick Wilson (1856–1930), an American linguist and scholar who devoted his life to proving the reliability of the Hebrew Bible, concluded the following after a lifetime of study in the Old Testament: "The result of my 45 years of study of the Bible has led me all the time to a firmer faith that in the Old Testament we have a true historical account of the history of the Israelite people."[15] As Josh McDowell concludes, "The Bible is unique in facing its critics. There is no book in all of literature like it. A person looking for truth would certainly consider a book that has the above qualifications."[16]

These things are just more of the many proofs that what is written in the Bible is God's Word and that it is true. Based on these three proofs, anyone should be convinced of the reliability of Scripture as it relates to uncovering the past events that have occurred, the present events that are currently occurring, and the future events that will occur.[17]

Chapter 2

What Happened Before Creation

Now that we have looked at the evidence for why the Bible is God's Word and is true, we will use quotes from Scripture to prove what happened on the earth after the time of creation. In Genesis 1:1, we read, "In the beginning God created the heavens and the earth." God existed prior to the creation of the earth, and He had created angels to serve Him and carry out His commands. Sometime prior to the creation of the earth, one of these angels, named Lucifer (also called Satan, the devil, the Evil One, the prince of the air, the Dragon, and other names), decided he would be God. Yet there is only one God, so the devil disobeyed God and sinned against Him, as the prophet Isaiah stated:

> How you are fallen from heaven, O Lucifer, son of the morning! How you are cut down to the ground, you who weakened the nations! For you have said in your heart: "I will ascend into heaven, I will exalt my throne above the stars of God; I will also sit on the mount of the congregation on the farthest side of the north; I will ascend above the heights of the clouds; I will be like the Most High."
>
> —Isaiah 14:12–14

Satan let his pride get the best of him and put himself before God, and anyone who does so will suffer the consequences. Satan's actions caused a war in heaven between those angels who chose to follow God and those who chose to follow Satan. In Revelation 12:7–9, John wrote, "War broke out in heaven: Michael and his angels fought with the dragon [Satan]; and the dragon and his angels fought, but they did not prevail, nor was a place found for them in heaven any longer. So the great dragon was cast out, that serpent of old, called the Devil and Satan, who deceives the whole world; he was cast to the earth, and his angels were cast out with him." Revelation 12:4 states, "His [Satan's] tail drew a third part of the stars [angels] of heaven and threw them to the earth." This indicates that there was a war in heaven and that a third of the angels God had created sinned and chose to follow Satan.

After the war in heaven, two-thirds of the angels remained on God's side, while one-third went to Satan's side. God had to separate the angels who chose to follow Satan from the ones who had remained faithful so He could punish those fallen angels later. If God had wanted to keep the same number of angels with Him in heaven, He could have chosen to do so; however, He would have had to provide some means to redeem them. This would have required Him to provide a perfect sacrifice each time the created angels sinned. Furthermore, if God had created more angels to take the place of the fallen ones who had sinned, those newly created angels would not have been given a choice about to whom they would serve. This could have led to another war in heaven, and the cycle could have been repeated.

God must have figured the cost of providing a perfect sacrifice for each created angel was too high, but He did not want any more wars in heaven, so He came up with an alternative plan of salvation. He decided to create one person, Adam, from whom would come the entire human race. In other words, God decided not to create new angels in heaven to replace the ones who had gone with Satan but instead, to create a new race of human beings on the earth. With one created being, God would only have to provide *one* perfect sacrifice in order to satisfy the debt of sin. As Paul stated in Romans 5:18–19:

> Therefore, as through one man's [Adam's] offense [sin] judgment came to all men, resulting in condemnation, even so through one Man's [Jesus Christ's] righteous act the free gift [of salvation] came to all men, resulting in justification of life. For as by one man's disobedience many were made sinners, so also by one Man's obedience many will be made righteous.

God's plan gave Adam and all of his descendants the choice to either follow God and spend eternity with Him in heaven or follow Satan and spend eternity with him in hell. In Chapter 8 we will examine in greater detail how one gets into heaven, but at this point, it is important to note that God does not want anyone in heaven who does not want to be there. He will never force Himself on anyone.

God developed this plan of salvation before the world was created. He created the world for human beings (see Genesis 1–2), and all humans living on earth must decide whether they want to live out eternity in heaven or hell. God then provided His only begotten Son, Jesus, to be the perfect sacrifice to redeem those human beings who chose to accept Him as their Savior. When Jesus died on the cross of Calvary, He paid the debt of sin that everyone owes but cannot pay. Those who put their trust in Jesus as their Savior will thus spend eternity in heaven, while those who do not put their trust in Jesus will spend eternity in hell.

Chapter 3

The Creation and Fall of Humanity

Now that God had His plan of salvation in place, He needed to provide the necessary elements to allow that plan to happen. First, He created the universe in which the human race would live (see Genesis 1). After God spoke the universe into existence, Satan and his fallen angels began living on the earth and in the space around the earth (this is why Satan is sometimes called the "prince of the power of the air"; see Ephesians 2:2). Then God created Adam, the first human. God provided Adam with a beautiful garden (the Garden of Eden) to live in and enjoy. The garden was perfect in every way, and everything was in harmony with God's purpose and plan.

God told Adam, "Of every tree of the garden you may freely eat; but of the tree of the knowledge of good and evil you shall not eat, for in the day that you eat of it you shall surely die" (Gen. 2:16–17). The Hebrew word translated "die" in this passage (*muwth*) means "to be separated from." In other words, God was telling Adam that if he ate of the fruit from the Tree of the Knowledge of Good and Evil, he would be separated from God. He did not mean Adam would physically die as we think of that word today.

Adam was not to be alone; God wanted him to have a helper. So God took one of Adam's ribs and made a woman, Eve (see Genesis 2:21–25). God blessed Adam and Eve and told them to populate the earth (see Genesis 1:28). As long as Adam and Eve remained obedient to God, they had a relationship and fellowship with God. At times, God would walk with Adam and Eve and talk directly with them.

Then one day, Satan came into the garden. Eve was looking at the Tree of the Knowledge of Good and Evil, and the fruit of the tree was appealing to her eye (see Genesis 3:6). Satan deceived Eve into eating of the fruit and disobeying (or sinning against) God. Eve then gave Adam some of the fruit, and he ate it as well (see Genesis 3:1–7). Satan enticed Eve to sin, and then Adam sinned knowingly. As Paul stated in 1 Timothy 2:13–14, "For Adam was formed first, then Eve. And Adam was not deceived, but the woman being deceived, fell into transgression [sin]."

In the same way that Satan sinned when he decided he wanted to be like God, Adam and Eve sinned when they decided they wanted to be like God and ate from the forbidden tree in the Garden of Eden. Sin broke the relationship and the fellowship. God could no longer walk and talk with them as He had before they had sinned, and He had to separate Himself from them. He threw Adam and Eve out of the Garden and placed cherubim at the entrance to make sure Adam and Eve could not get back in (see Genesis 3:23–24). They were thus prevented from eating of the Tree of Life, which, if they had been allowed to eat of it, would have given them eternal life.

Adam and Eve bore children and began to populate the earth God had created. In doing so, they passed their sin nature on to all of their descendants. Because of their sin, all of their descendants became sinners who fell short of getting into heaven. This means that every person born into the human race since the time of the Fall has a sinful nature that separates him or her from God. In Romans 3:23, Paul said, "For all [meaning every human being] have sinned and fall short of the glory of God." This sin nature is present from the time a person is conceived and continues for as long as he or she lives (see Psalm 51:5). It is this sin nature that makes it impossible for one to please God (see 1 John 3:8; Hebrews 7:7–10).

When Adam sinned, he became subject to the physical and spiritual death God had promised. When God promises good things, good things happen; but when He promises bad things, bad things happen. God always keeps His promises—every promise He has made has either been fulfilled or will be fulfilled. God loved Adam and Eve with an unconditional love, but He did not like what they had done in disobeying Him. In the same way, God loves each of us with an unconditional love, but He does not like for us to go outside of His will.

Human beings have both a physical and spiritual life. When a person dies a physical death, he or she no longer lives on the earth. That person's body is usually buried, but the spirit lives on for all eternity. Satan wants to keep people separated from God and out of heaven for all eternity, so he tries to deceive as many as he can into joining him. He does so by enticing each person to disobey God and reject Him. Satan cannot tell the truth. The best he can do is tell partial truths to deceive people (see John 8:44). Every person born into the human race is neutral about whether he or she will accept God's truth or Satan's lies. The choice is completely up to that individual.

As the earth became more and more populated, the human race continued to sin and disobey God. Genesis 6:1–2 states, "Now it came to pass, when men began to multiply on the face of the earth, and daughters were born to them, that the sons of God saw the daughters of men, that they were beautiful; and they took wives for themselves of all whom they chose." The term "sons of God" is most commonly understood to be the fallen angels who went with Satan (see also Job 1:6; 2:1). These fallen angels, in an attempt to prevent the virgin birth of Jesus and prevent God from providing a plan of salvation, were having children with human females. This was in direct contrast with God's order for the procreation of the human race.

When the Lord saw what was occurring on the earth, He decided to destroy every living creature upon it. Genesis 6:5–7 says, "Then the LORD saw that the wickedness of man [the whole human race] was great in the earth, and that every intent of the thoughts of his heart was only evil continually. The LORD was sorry that He made man on the earth, and He was grieved in His heart. So the LORD said, 'I will destroy man whom I have created from the face of the earth, both man and beast, creeping thing and birds of the air, for I am sorry that I have made them.'" For the moment, it seemed that Satan and his fallen angels had thwarted God's plans for the redemption of humankind.

Chapter 4

The Great Flood

When created angels sin, there is no way for them to restore the fellowship that once existed between them and God. Hebrews 2:16 says, "For indeed He [God] does not give aid to angels, but He does give aid to the seed of Abraham." This means that fallen angels have no means of spending eternity with God in heaven, because the Lord did not provide the means for them to do so.

As we read in the previous chapter, some of the fallen angels were indwelling human men and having children with human women. In other words, the fallen angels were not remaining in their proper domain. This was Satan's attempt to keep Jesus, the Son of God, from being born of a virgin. Ever since Satan sinned and fell from being an angel of God, he has tried to defeat God's plan of salvation for the world.

The human beings—the descendants of Adam and Eve—had one thought in mind: to do whatever they wanted to do whenever they wanted to do it without any regard to God. They were completely disobeying God and defying His purposes for those He desired to inhabit the earth. So God decided to destroy every living thing and start over (see Genesis 6:5–7). However, one man, Noah, "found grace [the unmerited love of God] in the eyes of the Lord" (Gen. 6:8). Noah was "a just man, perfect in his generations," and "walked with God" (Gen. 6:9).

The more individuals prosper, the less they tend to seek God and His ways in their lives. They become self-centered and self-sufficient, believing they are the ones responsible for their good fortune. When individuals (or nations) turn from God, He always warns them to come back before it is too late. He urges them to give up their sins, repent, and be restored to fellowship with Him. If they do not turn to Him, He punishes them in order to compel them to return. Then if they make the choice to come back to Him, He is always merciful. God wants to see that justice is done for all people and all nations. He wants people to live righteous lives according to His Word, the Bible.

The Bible states that at the time of Noah, "The earth also was corrupt before God, and the earth was filled with violence. So God looked upon the earth, and indeed it was corrupt; for all flesh had corrupted their way on the earth" (Gen. 6:11–12). The people in Noah's time were putting anything and everything ahead of God. They made idols out of things and worshiped them instead of God. As a result, God passed judgment on the inhabitants of the earth and condemned them to die because of their sin.

Many Americans today go about their lives as though nothing is wrong with their country, just as the people did in Noah's time. The United States is moving further and further away from God each day. If this trend continues, the nation will come to ruin and no longer be a strong power in this world. When people believe their nation is strong because of their own strength and turn from God, they are setting themselves up for a fall. It is God who makes nations strong, not those in the country. God is just as capable of making a sinful and evil nation weak as He is of making a righteous nation strong.

Three major categories of sins that have brought great nations down are (1) sins of the flesh, such as pride, illicit sex, gluttony, and disobedience to God; (2) partaking in vices, such as the use of liquor, beer, or drugs and other things that are not honoring to God; and (3) putting anything before God (in other words, idols). The United States is guilty of these sins, and this country is not an exception to God's sovereign will and ways. Will we be the next great nation to fall? Or will we stop our evil ways, repent, and turn to God so that He will have mercy on us?

When those in a nation violate God's laws, eventually they will suffer the consequences. God is a gracious and merciful God, slow to anger, abundant in lovingkindness, and relenting from doing harm (see Psalm 145:8–9); but at some point, His patience will run out, and the consequences for what was done will have to be paid. God will pour out His vengeance on every individual and nation who refuses to obey Him (see Micah 5:15). He requires people to do what is right in His sight, to love mercy, and to walk humbly with Him (see Micah 6:8). God acknowledges those who honor, obey, and serve Him.

It appears that Noah and his family were the only family on earth that was not affected by the demonic angels who were cohabiting with the human women. Noah was a man who believed in God as the creator of the universe and the only one who could save him from sin. He put his faith in God by obeying Him, and he was faithful to God in all areas of his life. Hebrews 11:7 says, "By faith Noah, being divinely warned of things not yet seen, moved with godly fear, prepared an ark for the saving of his household, by which he condemned the world and became heir of the righteousness which is according to faith." God used Noah to accomplish His purposes on the earth, selecting Noah to be the one through whom the human race would be saved from the flood.

Genesis 6:13 states, "God said to Noah, 'The end of all flesh has come before Me, for the earth is filled with violence through them; and behold, I will destroy them with the earth.'" God then told Noah to build an ark of gopher wood. He instructed Noah to make rooms in the ark; cover it inside and out with pitch; and make it 450 feet long, 75 feet wide, and 45 feet high (see Genesis 6:14–15). This would yield approximately 1.4 million cubic feet of space inside of the ark—large enough to contain all the animals God wanted Noah to take and all the supplies needed for those animals and Noah's family to survive. Noah was obedient to God. Genesis 6:22 says, "Thus Noah did; according to all that God commanded him, so he did."

It took Noah 120 long years to build the ark to God's specifications. During this time, Noah undoubtedly told the people about God, but the Bible does not record that anyone outside of his own family trusted in God.

Finally, when the ark was complete, the Lord said to Noah:

> "Come into the ark, you and all your household, because I have seen that you are righteous before Me in this generation. You shall take with you seven each of every clean animal, a male and a female; two each of animals that are unclean, a male and his female; also seven each of birds of the air, male and female, to keep the species alive on the face of all the earth. For after seven more days I will cause it to rain on the earth forty days and forty nights, and I will destroy from the face of the earth all living things I have made.
>
> —Genesis 7:1–4

Noah obeyed, and he, his wife, his sons, and his sons' wives went into the ark. God then caused it to rain for forty days and forty nights. The entire world was soon flooded with water, and the water remained on the earth for approximately 150 days. God took all of the fallen angels who had left their proper domain and locked them up so they could never again indwell the men of the earth or have children with the women. Jude 1:6 says, "The angels who did not keep their proper domain, but left their own abode, He [God] has reserved in everlasting chains under darkness for the judgment of the great day."

Note that it took Noah 120 years to build the ark and that during this time, the people of the earth could have turned to God and received His mercy. God is slow to get angry, but His power is unequaled, and He never lets those who disobey Him go without punishment (see Nahum 1:3). Often He will display His power in the difficult situations we experience in order to get our attention. He wants our obedience more than any gifts we could give to Him or any work we could do for Him. He wants us to spend time reading and studying His Word and talking with Him. He wants us to follow His will and purposes for our lives (see Hosea 6:6). If a person or nation turns to God, He will turn to them (see Zechariah 1:3). This means they must turn from their evil ways and give God their full focus, attention, minds, bodies, and souls. God takes revenge on all who oppose Him and furiously destroys

His enemies (see Nahum 1:2). Malachi 3:6 says, "For I [God] am the LORD, I do not change."

After the water receded, Noah and his family were returned to solid ground. God blessed Noah and his sons, and then He told them to do the same thing He had told Adam and Eve to do: "Be fruitful and multiply, and fill the earth" (Gen. 9:1). God always blesses those who are faithful and obedient to Him, but He never blesses those who are disobedient.

Now that God had locked up the fallen angels who had been having children with the human females, the earth began to be populated with the descendants of the human beings. The fallen angels were no longer able to prevent the virgin birth of Jesus by a human female. The people continued to increase and populate the earth, just as God had commanded Noah and his family.

God made each of us with the desire and ability to establish a relationship and fellowship with Him. He created us to love, obey, honor, and serve Him, but He gives us a choice as to whether we will accept Him or reject Him. God has made many promises to those of us who choose to trust Jesus as our Savior. However, the only way we can know those promises is to read and study His Word, the Bible.

Chapter 5

The Birth of the Nation of Israel

As the earth began to be populated with the descendents of the human beings, the people (who spoke only one language at the time) got together and decided to build a tower so tall it would allow them to enter heaven. The tower was called the *Tower of Babel.* God came down to see the city and the tower that these human beings were building, and He was not pleased with what the people were doing. So He confused their language and scattered them over the face of all the earth (see Genesis 11:1–9).

The people were trying to reach heaven through their own efforts, which is something none of us can do. In John 14:5–8, when Thomas said to Jesus, "Lord, we do not know where You are going, and how can we know the way?" Jesus replied, "I am the way, the truth, and the life. No one comes to the Father except through Me. If you had known Me, you would have known My Father also; and from now on you know Him and have seen Him." The only way for us to get to heaven is by trusting Jesus as our Savior. There is no one else or anything in the universe like God (see Deuteronomy 33:26). There is no other name given under heaven whereby we can be saved (See Acts 4:12).

Abram

God would orchestrate His own plan of redemption, and that plan involved a man named Abram. Abram lived in the ancient city of Ur, which was located in the land of the Chaldeans (modern-day Iraq). One day the Lord said to Abram, "Get out of your country, from your family and from your father's house, to a land that I will show you. I will make you a great nation; I will bless you and make your name great; and you shall be a blessing. I will bless those who bless you, and I will curse him who curses you; and in you all the families of the earth shall be blessed" (Gen. 12:1–3). God was calling Abram to be the head of a great nation for Himself so that Jesus, the Messiah, could be born of it. This nation would eventually be known as Israel.

In Romans 4:3, Paul wrote, "[Abram] believed God, and it was accounted to him for righteousness." Abram trusted God and was faithful, and he showed his faith by obeying God. He departed his land as the Lord had instructed, taking with him Sarai, his wife; Lot, his nephew; all the possessions that he had acquired in Ur; and all the servants he had acquired (see Genesis 12:4–6). Abram was seventy-five years old at the time.

When Abram arrived in the land of Canaan, the Lord appeared to him and said, "To your descendants I will give this land" (Gen. 12:7). Later, the Lord renewed His promise, saying,

> Lift your eyes now and look from the place where you are—northward, southward, eastward, and westward; for all the land which you see I give to you and your descendants forever. And I will make your descendants as the dust of the earth; so that if a man could number the dust of the earth, then your descendants also could be numbered. Arise, walk in the land through its length and its width, for I give it to you.
>
> —Genesis 13:14–17

God promised Abram that his descendants would be as the sands of the seashore so that no one could count them (see Genesis 22:17), but after some years had passed and Abram and Sarai still had no children, Sarai decided to "help" God by allowing her maidservant, Hagar, to bear a son to Abram. Abram agreed to the plan, and soon after, Hagar became pregnant. When the child was born, he was named Ishmael. Abram was eighty-six years old when Ishmael was born.

Of course, God does not need any help to accomplish what He has promised, nor does He bargain with anyone to accomplish His purposes. All God has to do is speak, and it will happen. God is in charge of the entire universe. In Romans 6:13, Paul tells us we are to use our entire bodies to honor and glorify God. This same God is the one who can give us eternal life in heaven with Him. God did not need any help in Abram's situation to do what He had promised. Abram and Sarai's attempts to help God failed, and they ended up causing pain and misery for themselves and for their descendants. As God told Hagar, her son would be "a wild man; his hand shall be against every man, and every man's hand against him. And he shall dwell in the presence of all his brethren" (Gen. 16:12).

Isaac

Years later, God appeared to Abram and said, "No longer shall your name be called Abram, but your name shall be Abraham; for I have made you a father of many nations.... As for Sarai your wife, you shall not call her name Sarai, but Sarah shall be her name" (Gen. 17:5, 15). At this time, Abraham was approximately ninety-nine years old, and Sarah was approximately eighty-nine years old. Genesis 18:11 states that both Abraham and Sarah were well-advanced in age and that Sarah had passed the age of childbearing. Yet in spite of their condition, God was still able to accomplish exactly what He said He would do.

It had been about twenty-five years since God had first told Abraham and Sarah they would have a son, but at last the promise would be fulfilled. "The LORD did for Sarah as He had spoken. For Sarah conceived and bore Abraham a son in his old age, at the set time which God had spoken to him. Abraham called the name of his son—whom Sarah bore to him—Isaac" (Gen. 21:1–3).

When God says an event will happen, He does not always tell us the exact time in which it will occur. God's timing is not our timing, but it is always perfect to accomplish His purpose and plan.

God made it clear to Abraham that Isaac was the son He had promised and it would be through Isaac that His promise of making Abraham into a great nation would be fulfilled. He told Abraham, "Do not let it be displeasing in your sight because of the lad [Ishmael] or because of your bondwoman [Hagar]. Whatever Sarah has said to you, listen to her voice; for in Isaac your seed shall be called. Yet I will also make a nation of the son of the bondwoman, because he is your seed" (Gen. 21:12–13). It would be through Israel that all the nations of the earth would be blessed (see Gen. 18:18). This blessing came as Jesus, the Messiah, as told in the New Testament.

Because of his attempts to "help" God, Abraham ended up being the father of two nations. The descendants of his first son, Ishmael, became the Ishmaelites, who are today known as the Arabs. The descendants of his promised son, Isaac, became the Israelites. These two nations have been at odds with each other for most of their history. All one has to do is read the headlines of the newspapers to see the continuing conflict occurring today in the Middle East between these two groups. One of the main conflicts is over the land God gave to Abraham and his descendents—a conflict that will continue until Jesus comes at the end of the tribulation period.

Today, it is evident that the promise God made to Abraham has been fulfilled. This one promise should be sufficient evidence that the Bible is true and is the Word of the living God. God can use anyone—regardless of his or her status, age, wealth, health, race, or any other human characteristic—to achieve His purposes on earth. The only thing that keeps God from using people to achieve His will is those people themselves. God will never use someone who refuses to let Him, because He will never force His will on anyone. God does not always seek out the best-qualified person for a job He wants done; He simply calls men and women who are willing to surrender themselves to Him and be faithful and obedient to Him no matter what.

Jacob

Isaac had twin sons: Esau and Jacob. Esau was the older son because he was born a few seconds before Jacob. In the culture of the time, the eldest son was usually favored because it was through him that the family was expanded. The eldest son inherited the majority of the family estate and received the blessings of the father, which were considered the "birthright" of the firstborn son. However, in Esau's case, he sold his birthright to his brother for a bowl of soup, and Jacob became the one through whom the nation of Israel would be established (see Genesis 25:24–34). Jacob had twelve sons: Reuben, Simeon, Levi, Judah, Issachar, Zebulun, Joseph, Benjamin, Dan, Naphtali, Gad, and Asher. These would become the fathers of the twelve tribes of Israel.

Joseph

While the other sons of Jacob were important, Joseph was the one whom God chose to save his entire family by moving them to Egypt. Joseph was not well liked by his brothers, but he was the favorite of his father, Jacob. Joseph's brothers were jealous of him, so they decided to get rid of Joseph by killing him. However, when they saw a passing caravan of Ishmaelites, who were headed to Egypt on a business trip, they decided to sell Joseph into slavery for twenty shekels of silver (see Genesis 37:19–28). Twenty shekels of silver equals approximately eight ounces, assuming a current price of silver of around six dollars per ounce. Joseph's brothers received about forty-eight dollars for him in today's money. This was a lot of money back in Joseph's time (approximately thirteen years of wages). Joseph's brothers reasoned that they would get some money and get rid of Joseph at the same time.

Joseph was around seventeen years old at the time. When he reached Egypt, he was sold as a slave to a man named Potiphar, who was captain of the guard for Pharaoh (see Genesis 39:1). Needless to say, Joseph was probably not happy to be a slave, but he had faith in God and trusted God to guide, protect, and watch over him. God gave Joseph good business judgment and blessed him because he was faithful and obedient to God no matter what the circumstances. Potiphar recognized Joseph's abilities and soon put Joseph in charge of all that he had. "Thus he [Potiphar] left all that he had in Joseph's hand, and he did not know what he had except for the bread which he ate" (Gen. 39:6).

Potiphar trusted Joseph so much that he did not even know how much wealth he had. His only concern was what food he would eat.

Joseph, with God's help, was successful at managing his master's business and household. He was also "handsome in form and appearance" (Gen. 39:6)—a fact that did not escape the notice of Potiphar's wife. After some time had passed, she began to make passes at Joseph to get him to sleep with her. "But he [Joseph] refused and said to his master's wife, 'Look, my master does not know what is with me in the house, and he has committed all that he has to my hand. There is no one greater in this house than I, nor has he kept back anything from me but you, because you are his wife. How then can I do this great wickedness, and sin against God?'" (Gen. 39:8–9).

Potiphar's wife continued to entice Joseph to sleep with her, but Joseph trusted God and stuck to his high morals. Time after time, Joseph continued to refuse her advances. This was probably a big blow to the ego of Potiphar's wife, so it seems that she made up her mind that if she could not have Joseph, no one else would. She devised a plan to put Joseph out of the house forever, where no one would be able to get him.

> But it happened about this time, when Joseph went into the house to do his work, and none of the men of the house were inside, that she [Potiphar's wife] caught him by his garment, saying, "Lie with me." But he left his garment in her hand, and fled and ran outside. And so it was, when she saw that he had left his garment in her hand and fled outside, that she called to the men of her house and spoke to them, saying, "See, he [Potiphar] has brought in to us a Hebrew [Joseph] to mock us. He [Joseph] came in to me to lie with me, and I cried out with a loud voice. And it happened, when he heard that I lifted my voice and cried out, that he left his garment with me, and fled and went outside."
>
> —Genesis 39:11–15

When Potiphar came home, his wife told her version of what had happened. Potiphar became jealous and angry, and in the heat of the moment, he had Joseph put in prison (see Genesis 39:19–20). In a similar way, when we act out of anger without first getting all of the facts, it typically leads us to a wrong conclusion. Our anger leads to us making flawed decisions, just as Potiphar made. For Joseph's part, he was simply doing his best to be faithful and obedient to God. He wanted to be what God wanted him to be and was willing to be used by God to accomplish His purposes. It is when we are faithful and obedient to God, that Satan will attack the hardest in our lives.

Looking back on his life, Joseph couldn't say it had been all that good according to the world's standards. One could even say his life had been a series of bad things happening to a good person. He had been betrayed by his brothers, taken to a foreign country, sold to Potiphar as a slave, set up for attempted rape by Potiphar's wife, and now thrown into prison. He probably asked, "Why me, Lord? What have I done to deserve all that is happening to me?" Yet through it all, Joseph trusted in God and put his faith in God to guide and direct him. God knew Joseph's heart, and He had not forgotten about him.

The prisons in that time were not what they are today. In fact, the prisons of today would have been considered luxurious compared to the one in which Joseph was placed. Prisoners today have air conditioning, heat, running water, restrooms, good food, medical attention when needed, access to visitors, and even TV and recreation facilities. They have rights and don't have to worry about cruel and unusual punishment. In Joseph's time, prisoners were beaten, fed little, sometimes worked to death, and generally treated as scum. Even though Joseph's jailer liked him and gave Joseph special favors, it did not make the prison come anywhere close to what he would have experienced today.

While Joseph was in prison, Pharaoh's chief butler and chief baker offended him, and he had both of them thrown into the prison where Joseph was (see Genesis 40:1–3). Both the chief butler and the chief baker had a trusted position with the king and were his loyal subjects. While they were in prison, each man had a dream about what was going to happen to him. So they came to Joseph with their dreams and asked him to interpret them. Joseph said to the men, "Do not interpretations belong to God? Tell them to me, please" (Gen. 40:8).

When the chief butler related his dream, Joseph told him that within three days he would be restored to his high office in Pharaoh's service. Joseph asked the chief butler to speak to Pharaoh on his behalf, telling him that he had been stolen from the land of the Hebrews and had done nothing to deserve being put in prison. In other words, he wanted the chief butler to see if he could get him out of prison (see Genesis 40:9–15).

The chief baker, seeing the positive interpretation of the chief butler's dream, also told Joseph his dream. This time, the interpretation did not prove as favorable. In fact, Joseph told the chief baker that within three days, Pharaoh would have him killed (see Genesis 40:16–19). This is one of the few instances in which a person has known exactly how much time he or she had to live. No one can guarantee that he or she will have even fifteen seconds more to live. Life is uncertain, and yet we live as though we have years left to make decisions we have put off time and time again.

Both of the interpretations came true. The chief butler was restored to his position, while the chief baker died by hanging. Unfortunately, when the chief butler was restored to his high position by Pharaoh, he forgot all about Joseph (see Genesis 40:20–23). Joseph would have to wait in prison for two more long years before something would change his situation. That would be enough to make anyone discouraged—but not Joseph.

One day, this same pharaoh had a series of dreams and was so troubled by them that he called in all of his wise men and magicians to interpret them. Yet none of these men could tell Pharaoh what the dreams were about (see Genesis 41:1–8). Then the chief butler remembered that a man named Joseph had once interpreted his and the chief baker's dreams while they were in prison and that those dreams had both been fulfilled. He told Pharaoh about Joseph and his accurate interpretations of the dreams, and Pharaoh summoned Joseph to appear at his court (see Genesis 41:9–14).

When Joseph arrived, Pharaoh said to him, "I have had a dream, and there is no one who can interpret it. But I have heard it said of you that you can understand a dream, to interpret it" (Gen. 41:15).

Joseph replied, "It is not in me; God will give Pharaoh an answer of peace" (Gen. 41:16).

Notice that Joseph told Pharaoh *he* did not have the answer but *God* did and that God would give Pharaoh the answer through him. Despite all of the difficulties Joseph had endured, he still trusted in

God for the answers. He knew that the true answer would come only from God. So Pharaoh told Joseph the two dreams. When he finished, Joseph told Pharaoh the two dreams were one and the same. He then gave the following interpretation:

> The seven good cows are seven years, and the seven good heads of corn are seven years; the dreams are one. And the seven thin and ugly cows which came up after them are seven years, and the seven empty heads blighted by the east wind are seven years of famine. This is the thing which I have spoken to Pharaoh. God has shown Pharaoh what He is about to do. Indeed seven years of great plenty will come throughout all the land of Egypt; but after them seven years of famine will arise, and all the plenty will be forgotten in the land of Egypt; and the famine will deplete the land. So the plenty will not be known in the land because of the famine following, for it will be very severe. And the dream was repeated to Pharaoh twice because the thing is established by God, and God will shortly bring it to pass.
>
> —Genesis 41:26–32

The dreams indicated a course of action Pharaoh needed to take to preserve the land during a period of famine. Joseph then told Pharaoh that he should select an intelligent and discerning person to place over the food production of Egypt (see Genesis 41:33–36). The plan Pharaoh would put in place would allow Egypt and the surrounding countries affected by the famine to survive. To this, Pharaoh replied, "Inasmuch as God has shown you all this, there is no one as discerning and wise as you. You shall be over my house, and all my people shall be ruled according to your word; only in regard to the throne will I be greater than you.... See I have set you over all the land of Egypt" (Gen. 41:39–41).

Joseph had gone from riches to rags, rags to riches, riches to rags (and prison), and now rags to riches again. His life had been so up and down during his short years on earth that he must have felt he was on some kind of rollercoaster. This time, he was given a high-ranking position in the Egyptian government, second only to Pharaoh. Joseph was about thirty years old when Pharaoh set him over all the land of Egypt. God had a purpose and plan for Joseph, and He intended to fulfill it in spite of all the problems Joseph had encountered in his life.

The famine came, just as God said it would. By this time, Joseph had been stockpiling food for seven years, and now he opened the storehouses of Egypt (see Genesis 41:53–57). When the famine struck Canaan, Jacob heard that there was food in Egypt and sent his sons to see if they could purchase some for the family (see Genesis 42:1–2). After a long series of events, Joseph was eventually reunited with his brothers and forgave them for selling him into slavery. He told them, "So now it was not you who sent me here, but God; and He has made me a father to Pharaoh, and lord of all his house, and a ruler throughout all the land of Egypt" (Gen. 45:8).

Jacob and all of his family, the descendants of Abraham, moved from Canaan to Goshen in Egypt so that they would have the necessities of life and survive the terrible famine throughout the area (see Gen. 46:5–7). Once Jacob and all of his family had been reunited in Goshen, Joseph reassured his brothers that he held no grudge against them. He told them, "Do not be afraid, for am I in the place of God? But as for you, you meant evil against me; but God meant it for good, in order to bring it about as it is this day, to save many people alive. Now therefore, do not be afraid; I will provide for you and your little ones" (Gen. 50:19–21). Joseph comforted his brothers and spoke kindly to them.

What a great example Joseph's life is to those who are faithful and obedient to God! It was not always an easy road for Joseph, but God was with him all the time and was working out His purpose and plan. Not once did Joseph try to get even with the butler for waiting two years to tell Pharaoh about his being in prison. After his release, even though he was of a higher rank than Potiphar, he did not try to get even with his former master or his wife, who had falsely accused him. He also completely forgave his brothers, who had sold him into slavery, and did not hold anything against them.

Joseph moved his entire family from the land of Canaan to Egypt around 1845 B.C. Genesis ends with the death of Joseph at the age of 110, which occurred around 1804 B.C. (see Genesis 50:26). This does not end the history of Israel, but it brings the life of Joseph to a close.

Chapter 6

The Exodus

Approximately 135 years before Joseph was born, God had said to Abraham, "Know certainly that your descendants will be strangers in a land that is not theirs, and will serve them, and they will afflict them four hundred years" (Gen. 15:13). God told Abraham that his descendents would spend 400 years in a foreign country and would serve that country's people as slaves—a prophecy that was ultimately fulfilled during the time of Moses. For many people, this alone is enough proof that the Bible is true and the Word of God. No person past or present has been able to predict accurately what will take place 135 years before it happens and have it fulfilled exactly as told. The fulfillment of this prophecy also points to the fact that God always keeps His promises, no matter how many years have passed since He first made them.

A New Pharaoh

As time passed, the events of Joseph's life and what he had done to save Egypt and the surrounding countries from the famine were slowly forgotten. During the next three hundred years after his death, the

Israelites multiplied and became a numerous population group in Egypt. By 1504 B.C., this had come to the attention of a new Pharaoh in Egypt.

> Now there arose a new king [Pharaoh] over Egypt, who did not know Joseph. And he said to his people, "Look, the people of the children of Israel are more and mightier than we; come, let us deal shrewdly with them, lest they multiply, and it happen, in the event of war, that they also join our enemies and fight against us, and so go up out of the land." Therefore, they [the Egyptians] set taskmasters over them [the children of Israel] to afflict them with their burdens. And they built for Pharaoh supply cities, Pithom and Raamses. But the more they afflicted them [the children of Israel], the more they multiplied and grew. And they [the Egyptians] were in dread of the children of Israel. So the Egyptians made the children of Israel serve with rigor. And they made their lives bitter with hard bondage—in mortar, in brick, and in all manner of service in the field. All their service in which they made them serve was with rigor.
>
> —Exodus 1:8–14

The children of Abraham lived in Egypt from approximately 1845 B.C. to 1445 B.C. The Egyptians began to make slaves of the Israelites in 1504 B.C. and continued until the exodus in 1445 B.C. The Israelites were thus in slavery for a period of fifty-nine years. During the four hundred years the family of Jacob lived in Egypt, the nation of Israel grew to about 603,000 males. This number did not include women and children—if they had been included in the count, the number of Israelites would have been around two million. The new pharaoh who came to power perceived this large group of people living in Goshen to be a threat to the land of Egypt and its world power, and he began to take measures to enslave and subjugate the people to eliminate this threat.

However, no matter what Pharaoh or the Egyptians did to the children of Israel, they continued to multiply. They became a larger and stronger population in Goshen, just as God had planned. Finally, Pharaoh commanded the Egyptians to kill all of the male children born to the children of Israel (see Exodus 1:16–22). This is the first recorded instance in the Bible of a nation killing babies or persecuting the Jewish people.

The Calling of Moses

It was at this time that a child named Moses was born. His mother, an Israelite, hid him for three months so he would not be discovered by the Egyptians and drowned in the Nile. When she could no longer hide Moses, she put him in a waterproof basket and placed the basket in the river near the spot where Pharaoh's daughter came to bathe. Moses' sister stood a short distance away to see that no harm would come to Moses (see Exodus 2:1–4).

Pharaoh's daughter found Moses in the basket and had compassion on him. She decided to raise him as her son, and it was she who actually gave him the name "Moses." Moses thus survived the killing of the male babies as the son of Pharaoh's daughter. He was educated and raised as Pharaoh's grandson (see Exodus 2:5–10).

Moses had great leadership skills, and he eventually found his real mother and father among the Hebrew slaves. Then one day, Moses saw an Egyptian beating one of the Hebrew people, and he killed the Egyptian and buried him in the sand. The next day, fearing his crime had been discovered, he fled from Egypt to save his life. Moses eventually arrived in Midian. After Moses married Zipporah and spent forty years in Midian tending the sheep of Jethro, his father-in-law, God called Moses to lead His people out of Egyptian bondage (see Exodus 2:11–25).

One day when Moses was out taking care of the sheep, he saw a bush that was on fire, but the fire did not consume the bush as it should. This unusual sight got his attention, so he went over to get a closer look at this strange phenomenon. As he approached, God spoke from the center of the burning bush. He told Moses to take off his shoes, because the ground he was standing on was holy.

This is the way it should always be when we approach God in prayer. We should act as though we are on holy ground, because we are in the very presence of God. God is listening to our every word, and He wants us to obey Him so He can bless us. Yet God will only do this if we allow Him to do so. In order to walk and talk with God, we must humble ourselves before Him.

God told Moses he was to lead the children of Israel out of Egypt and into the Promised Land of Canaan (see Exodus 3:1–10). Moses was approximately eighty years old when God called him to lead His people out of Egypt. At first, he made all kinds of excuses to get out of doing what God had told him to do (see Exodus 3:11–4:17). In the same way, when God calls us to do something, we often make as many excuses as we possibly can for not doing what is required of us. Of course, Moses had a compelling reason for not going back: it could cost him his life. Yet God eventually convinced him to return to Egypt and lead His people out of bondage. God told Moses to take his brother, Aaron, with him to speak for him (see Exodus 4:18–31).

The Escape from Egypt

When Moses and Aaron arrived in Egypt, they asked Pharaoh as nicely as they could to let the Israelites go some distance away to worship God. Pharaoh refused, so God upped the stakes and began to pour out plagues upon Egypt. Each plague increased in intensity and was stronger and more devastating than the previous one (see Exodus 5–10).

Finally, after nine plagues had been poured out, God inflicted the tenth and final plague on the Egyptians: the death of the firstborn. God instructed the Israelites to sprinkle the blood of a lamb on their doorposts so that the plague would "pass over" their households (see Exodus 11–12:30). The Egyptians had killed the male Hebrew babies in order to keep the Israelites from becoming strong, and now God was showing Egypt that this was not a wise thing to do. God loves all the children of the world. In Luke 18:16, Jesus says, "Let the little children come to Me, and do not forbid them; for of such is the kingdom of God."

After this tenth plague, Pharaoh agreed to let God's people go so they could worship their God. However, he quickly changed his mind once the Israelites had left Egypt, and he led his superior army, consisting of six hundred of the nation's best chariots, in pursuit of the

Israelites. When he reached the Israelites' encampment at Pi Hahiroth, he thought he had the children of Israel trapped. With the Red Sea in front of the Israelites and the Egyptian army behind them, it seemed the Israelites had no chance of escape (see Exodus 12:31–14:12).

This situation would make even the strongest person feel discouraged and helpless. The Israelites had no military experience, no weapons, and no way to defend themselves. However, when God makes a plan, it is perfect; and He will accomplish that plan, even if we do not understand how it will happen. In the Israelites' case, God worked a huge miracle by putting an angel behind the Israelites so that the Egyptian army could not reach them. Then God parted the waters of the Red Sea, and the children of Israel walked across on dry land. After the Israelites had crossed the Red Sea, God removed the angel that had been protecting the Israelites. When Pharaoh's army rode into the Red Sea to pursue the Israelites, God released the waters, and the entire Egyptian army was killed (see Exodus 14:13–31).

Remember that the children of Israel had been in Egypt the required four hundred years that God had told Abraham his descendents would spend in a foreign country. This amazing prophecy given so long ago to Abraham had now been fulfilled. As previously stated, there were approximately two million people (including the women and children) who crossed the Red Sea on dry land, and they were witnesses that this event had actually happened.

Mount Sinai and Instructions for the Tabernacle

Even though the children of Israel had been saved from the Egyptians, they still had to cross several countries to get to the Promised Land. After a few months, the Israelites arrived at a placed called Rephidim, where God miraculously provided water for them from a rock. There, they were attacked by a group of people known as the Amalekites. The Amalekites were descendents of Esau, Jacob's twin brother. God defeated the Amalekites on the Israelites' behalf (see Exodus 17:1–13).

The Israelites ultimately arrived at Mount Sinai, where God gave Moses the Ten Commandments and His law (see Exodus 20–24). God gave instructions to Moses for making the tabernacle, the ark of the covenant, the table of showbread, the lamp stand, and the altar of burnt offering (see Exodus 25–27). He also gave Moses instructions on how to make the garments for the priesthood. Aaron was consecrated to be the high priest, and his sons were to minister as priests. The priests were responsible for taking care of the tabernacle and its furniture, fixtures, and utensils and for performing all of the sacrifices required by God (see Exodus 28–29).

God then gave Moses further instructions concerning the building of the tabernacle, additional furniture and fixtures for the tabernacle, and priestly garments (see Exodus 30–40). Moses had the tabernacle, the furniture to go in the tabernacle, and all of the garments made according to God's instructions. In the tabernacle was a special room called *the inner sanctuary,* or *the Most Holy Place,* where the presence of God stayed among His people. The book of Leviticus records information about this and the laws about the offerings and sacrifices that God gave to Moses in great detail. God told Moses exactly how the priests were to handle each situation, sacrifice, and offering.

The Census and Provisions for the People

Two years after the Israelites left Egypt, God told Moses to take a census of the people:

> The LORD spoke to Moses in the Wilderness of Sinai, in the tabernacle of meeting, on the first day of the second month, in the second year after they had come out of the land of Egypt, saying: "Take a census of all the congregation of the children of Israel, by their families, by their fathers' houses, according to the number of names, every male individually, from twenty years old and above—all who are able to go to war in Israel. You and Aaron shall number them by their armies."
>
> —Numbers 1:1–3

The census revealed that there were 603,550 men who were at least twenty years of age and able to fight in the army, not counting the members of the tribe of Levi, who were the priests and were dedicated to serving God (see Numbers 1:44–47). This is the same number recorded in Exodus 38:26, which means that none of the men who had come out of Egypt had died. This census also allowed the Israelites to rearrange and register the people according to their tribes.

The Israelites left Mount Sinai, and God directed them on their way. By day, God led the Israelites with a cloud over the tabernacle; by night, He guided them with a pillar of fire. When the cloud or the pillar moved from over the tabernacle, the Israelites were to follow. When it stood still, the Israelites were to make camp. This cloud and pillar of fire were large enough for approximately two million people to see them and obey God (see Numbers 9:15–23).

The logistics of moving two million people from east of the Red Sea to the land of Canaan were tremendous, and getting enough food and water for the people was an unending task. There were no paved roads, no maps, no trucks or buses, and no other modern conveniences we use today to get from one place to another. Some of the people had wagons, but most of them had to walk and carry their possessions or use pack animals. The animals had to be fed and watered as well. This was no easy task for Moses to accomplish, but his faith in God carried him through.

Because there were no markets in the desert or in the wilderness, it was a continuous job for Moses to find food and water for the people and the animals. Eventually, God provided manna for the Israelites, and from time to time, He provided water for them. Manna was the perfect food and provided all the necessary nutrients and vitamins needed to sustain life and maintain a healthy body. Yet the people got tired of the same old diet day after day and complained to God, so out of His loving and compassionate mercy and grace, He sent quail for the people to eat (see Exodus 16; Numbers 11:4–32).

The Israelites Arrive at the Promised Land

The children of Israel, following God's leading, arrived at the Wilderness of Paran and set up camp. The Israelites were a large group of people that would attract the attention of any country close to where they camped. God soon told Moses to select twelve men—one from each of the twelve tribes—to go out and explore the land. These men were to go into Canaan, the land God had promised to Abraham and his descendants, and investigate it to determine how best to take it (see Numbers 13:1–2). God had already given the land of Canaan to the Israelites, so all they had to do was go in and take it.

Moses followed God's directions. He selected one man from each of the twelve tribes and told them to go into the land and then report back about what they found. These twelve men traveled throughout the land of Canaan as instructed and reported back to the people. Two of the men, Caleb and Joshua, stated that Canaan was a great and prosperous land. Caleb told the people, "Let us go up at once and take possession, for we are well able to overcome it" (Num. 13:30).

The other ten men agreed that it was a great and prosperous land, but they said there were giants living there and that the Israelites could not possibly take it. "The land through which we have gone as spies is a land that devours its inhabitants," they said, "and all the people whom we saw in it are men of great stature. There we saw the giants (the descendants of Anak came from the giants); and we were like grasshoppers in our own sight, and so we were in their sight" (Num. 13:32–33).

Thus, the Israelites disobeyed God and refused to take the land He had given them. They would rather have returned to Egypt as slaves than be free and occupy an ideal land God had provided (see Numbers 14:1–4). Today, we often prefer to be slaves to sin rather than experience God's wonderful blessings. When we are on God's side and are faithful and obedient to His purposes and will, we become victorious, because nothing can prevail against God's sovereign will.

Often we look on the circumstances and get discouraged and downtrodden when what we really need to do is keep our eyes focused on the true and living God and trust Him to keep His promises. That is what happened to the Israelites. They looked at the circumstances, took their eyes off God, doubted Him, trusted in their own strength to conquer the land of Canaan, and disobeyed Him. Any nation or individual who does not obey God will always suffer the consequences of disobedience. Sometimes God does not carry out the consequences of disobedience immediately, but rest assured, those consequences will come.

Because the Israelites disobeyed God by refusing to take possession of the land, they suffered the consequences. God pronounced a physical death sentence on all the people who were numbered in the first census, except for Moses, Caleb, and Joshua. In fact, God was so angry with the people for not entering the land of Canaan that at first He was going to wipe out every one of them and start a new nation with Moses. But Moses interceded for the people in prayer, and God decided to kill only those people who were twenty years old and older so they would never enter the Promised Land (see Numbers 14:11–35).

When Moses told the people what God had said, they quickly decided to reverse their decision. Despite Moses' warning that they had made their choice and there was nothing they could do to change it, the Israelites decided to attack the Amalekites and Canaanites and take the land. Moses told the people they would be defeated—God had made His decision, and the people would have to suffer the consequences—but they rejected Moses' advice and attacked the Amalekites who lived in the hill country. As Moses had said, the Amalekites and Canaanites easily defeated the Israelites (see Numbers 14:39–45). When we bargain with God, God always wins.

Wandering in the Wilderness

The Israelites now had no choice but to wander around in the wilderness until all the people on whom God had pronounced His judgment were dead. This would take approximately forty years. After this time, God would lead the remaining people into the promised land of Canaan. As the people began to wander in the wilderness, God gave instructions for the tithes and offerings the people would give to Him (see Numbers 15).

There was much discontent among the people throughout the forty years they wandered in the wilderness. They suffered hunger, thirst, plagues, sicknesses and other discomforts, and many times they complained bitterly to Moses. During one such occasion, a man named Korah (a Levite) gathered 250 leaders of the Israelites to oppose the authority of Moses and Aaron. He said to Moses, "You take too much upon yourselves, for all the congregation is holy, every one of them, and the LORD is among them. Why then do you exalt yourselves above the assembly of the LORD?" (Num. 16:3).

God dealt with these rebels and reaffirmed His choice of Moses, Aaron, and the priests He had selected by splitting the ground apart under the tents of Korah and his followers. The next day, when the Israelites complained about what had happened, God sent a plague that killed 14,700 of the people before Moses could make atonement for them (see Numbers 16:23–49). God was displeased that the people did not trust and obey Him. He gave them more laws and commandments concerning the duties of the priests and the laws of purification around this time (see Numbers 18–19). Shortly thereafter, Aaron died; and Eleazar, his son, became the high priest (see Numbers 20:22–29).

At a place called Kadesh, there was again no water for the people, and they complained to Moses about the situation. Some even stated that they wished they had died in Egypt rather than in the desert. God told Moses to gather the people together and speak to a rock, and water would come forth. But Moses' anger caused him to disobey God, and instead of speaking to the rock, Moses struck it with his rod. Because Moses disobeyed the Lord, he was not allowed to enter the land of Canaan (see Numbers 20:1–12). Nations and individuals who do not obey God will suffer the consequences at the time He determines—not sooner or later, but exactly at the time God determines.

Beginning the Conquest

After the Israelites had wandered around in the desert for forty years and all the people whom God had said would die had died, it was now time—according to God's timetable—for the Israelites to go into the land of Canaan and possess it. However, because the Israelites had been slaves in Egypt and not soldiers, God first had to give them some experience in warfare so that they would gain confidence in their ability to conquer the land. God gave the Israelites some strange battle strategies that a hardened general would laugh at and never use. One of the strange battle strategies was when God told Joshua to take the city of Jericho, which was heavily protected by a large wall. God had seven priests and the army march around Jericho each day for six days. Then on the seventh day, the priests and the army marched around Jericho seven times, and as the priests blew the trumpet in obedience to God's command, the walls fell to the ground. The Israelites easily defeated Jericho.

As the Israelites moved from Mount Hor toward the land of Canaan, they were attacked by the Canaanites, who lived in the south. God delivered up the Canaanites, and the Israelites completely destroyed them and all of their cities.

The Israelites then moved from Mount Hor to the country of Moab. On the way, the Israelites approached the country of the Amorites and requested permission to pass through their land. The Israelites promised they would not destroy or plunder the country and would stay on the established travel routes. When the Israelites came to pass through Edom, the Israelites even agreed to pay the going price for all that they needed (see Numbers 20:14–19). However, Sihon, the king of the Amorites, refused to let the people pass through the land and gathered his army together to attack the Israelites (see Numbers 21:21–26). God was again with the Israelites, and they soundly defeated the Amorites. The Israelites occupied the Amorites' land and began to plan the conquest of the other nations that were between them and Canaan (see Numbers 21:1–3, 10–13, 21–26).

Even in those days, when the only communication system was "tell-a-person," news of a large invasion force spread quickly. King Og of Bashan heard about the success of the Israelites and decided to attack them. God again used the Israelite army, and they defeated the king of Bashan (see Numbers 21:33–35). By now, the Israelites had gained confidence and had increased their trust in God and His strength to accomplish His goals and purposes. It was not through their strength that they would conquer and live in the land of Canaan but through God's.

The Israelites moved into the plains of Moab and camped on the east side of the Jordan River, across from the city of Jericho. Balak, king of the Moabites, saw what the Israelites had done to the Amorites and joined forces with the Midianites to attack and defeat the Israelites. After some time had elapsed and they had engaged in discussions with a man named Balaam, the Moabites and Midianites became convinced that God was with the Israelites and went home (see Numbers 22–24).

While the Israelites were camped in the plains of Moab, God told Moses to conduct another census of the people. As you may recall, the first census Moses had taken indicated that the total number of men was 603,550 (see Numbers 1:14–46). The new census indicated that the total number of men was 601,730—1,820 fewer men (see Numbers 26).

During their stay in the land of Moab, God also gave the Israelite people several more laws and commanded more offerings. He also named Joshua as the next leader. He would take over after Moses died (Num. 27–30).

God told Moses to take vengeance on the Midianites because they were responsible for causing the Israelites to sin at Peor (see Numbers 25). So the Israelites attacked the Midianites and killed all the males as well as all the females who were not virgins. Then the Israelites divided the plunder among themselves (see Numbers 31). At this point, two of the tribes (the Reubenites and Gadites) decided to settle east of the Jordan River instead of taking part in the conquest of the land of Canaan to the west of the Jordan River. However, these tribes promised to fight with the other tribes until the land was secured (see Numbers 32).

Final Preparations for Entering Canaan

The Israelites were now ready to take possession of the Promised Land. However, before they entered the land, Moses wanted to call the people together to remind them of everything the Lord had commanded them after they left Egypt. The book of Deuteronomy contains Moses' final instructions to the Israelites about what God wanted His people to do and observe. Moses reviewed the Ten Commandments, cautioned the people against disobeying God, reminded them that they were God's chosen people, told them that obedience to God brought blessings, warned them against false gods, and instructed them on many other issues related to worshiping and serving God (see Deuteronomy 1–31). He reminded them God was not created for man; rather, man was created by God for God.

Moses' final act was to bless the tribes of Israel (see Deuteronomy 33). It is interesting to note that Moses did not bless the tribe of Simeon. Simeon was the tribe that had lost the most men from the time of the first census to the time of the second census—37,100 men during the forty years of wandering in the wilderness (see Numbers 1:23; 26:14).

After giving the blessings, Moses went to Mount Nebo, where he was allowed to view the land of Canaan. There Moses died, never to enter the Promised Land because he had disobeyed God by not speaking to the rock for water as God had commanded. Moses was 120 years old at the time of his death, yet he had not lost any of his physical capacity (see Deuteronomy 34).

God provided everything the Israelites needed at the proper time to get them out of their slavery in Egypt. All they had to do was obey God and trust in Him. God always knows what is best for each of His family members, and He will provide it at the exact time it is needed.

Chapter 7

The Rise and Fall of Israel

After the death of Moses, the leadership of Israel passed to Joshua. Joshua was faithful and obedient to God. He had been one of the two spies (along with Caleb) who had voted to take the land of Canaan in spite of the circumstances that appeared to be overwhelmingly against Israel.

God told Joshua to attack the city of Jericho first and gave him instructions on how to defeat it (see Joshua 1–2). The Israelites crossed the Jordan River while God miraculously held back the floodwaters, just as He had done at the Red Sea, and Israel entered into the Promised Land (see Joshua 3). The Israelites defeated the people of Jericho and killed every person in the city except Rahab, who had previously helped the Israelite spies, and her family (see Joshua 5:13–6:27).

The Conquest Is Completed

The news of the defeat of Jericho spread quickly throughout the surrounding lands. The Israelites looked unstoppable; but unknown to Joshua, sin had entered the Israelite camp. When Joshua attacked the city of Ai, he was defeated, and thirty-six Israelites were killed. These are the first known Israelite casualties of the war to capture the Promised Land. Joshua was upset over the defeat, and he tore his clothes and pleaded with the Lord to preserve the people (see Joshua 7:1–9).

God answered by revealing to Joshua that a man named Achan had disobeyed Him and sinned. This was the cause of Israel's defeat. So, at God's command, the people annihilated the entire family of Achan, and after this, they again attacked the people of Ai. This time the Lord was with the Israelites, and they defeated Ai (see Joshua 7:10–8). This is an important lesson for us: When we sin, we not only cause suffering to ourselves but also to others.

Joshua 9–12 tells how the Israelites went on to conquer the rest of the nations that were occupying the land of Canaan. When the victory was complete, the land was divided among the remaining ten tribes (remember that two of the tribes had settled east of the Jordan River). The tribe of Levi was not given any land, as they represented the priests, but they were given places to live among the other twelve tribes (see Joshua 13–21). After this, the Reubenites and Gadites, who had supported the other tribes in the conflict, returned to their lands to the east of the Jordan (see Joshua 22).

The Period of the Judges Over Israel

It took many years for the Israelites to secure the land of Canaan, and by the time the conquest was nearly complete Joshua was well-advanced in years. In Joshua 23–24, he gives the people one last address, after which, he dies. As the book of Joshua comes to a close, the high priest, Eleazar, son of Aaron, also dies.

As long as Joshua and the elders who outlived Joshua were alive, the people served and obeyed the one and only true and living God. However, after these leaders died, the people began to go astray and disobey God. Each person began to do what seemed right to him or her and ignored God (see Judges 2). This always is a huge mistake. It caused the entire nation to stray from God.

God expected the people to trust and obey Him for direction and guidance, but they continued to disobey and reject Him as their leader. The same is often true of us today. Whenever things are going our way, we tend to think they came about as a result of our own doing. We begin to trust in our own strength rather than in God's wisdom and seek to accomplish our goals instead of His. This is never a good strategy, because only God can see what the future holds for us.

The Israelites entered into a period of approximately 350 years, during which, from time to time, God called various people to lead the Israelites. This duration of time is called *the period of judges*, and it is marked by a cycle of events, as follows:

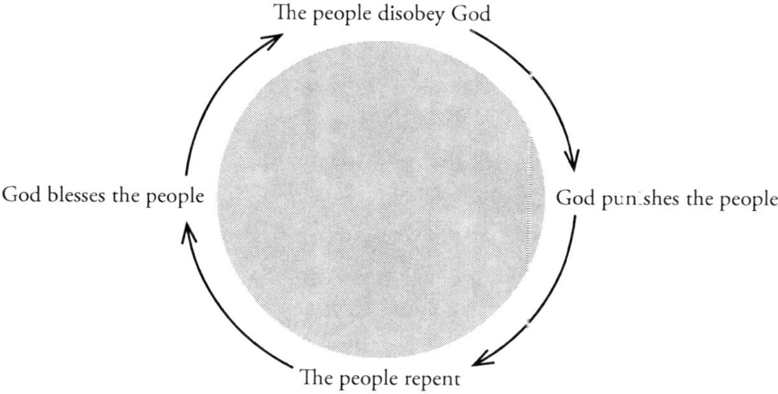

After this cycle of disobedience, punishment, repentance, and blessing concluded, the people would begin to disobey again, and the cycle would start over. Today, as nations and individuals, we often go through this same cycle.

The Period of the Kings Over Israel

The people's final rejection of God as their leader came while Samuel was judge of Israel. When he grew old, the Israelites came to him and demanded to have a king just like all the other countries in the region. When Samuel prayed to the Lord about the request, God replied, "Heed the voice of the people in all that they say to you; for they have not rejected you, but they have rejected Me, that I should not reign over them" (1 Sam. 8:7).

God told Samuel to select Saul as the first king of Israel, and at first, Saul did a good job. However, one day the Philistines gathered an army of thirty thousand chariots and six thousand horsemen against Saul. Samuel told Saul he was to wait for Samuel to come and make an offering to God, but Saul got tired of waiting and made the burnt offering himself. When Samuel arrived, he told Saul he had acted foolishly. He told Saul he had disobeyed God, and for this, he would lose the leadership of God's people (see 1 Samuel 13:1–15).

So often we want things done our way instead of God's. We seem to be living in a "now" generation—we want everything done this instant, in our timeframe. However, when we forget that God's timing is always perfect and do things in our own way, we miss the blessings God has for us. God is the only one who can see the past, present, and future at the same time, and He always has the best for us in mind—even though it might not look like it at the time. In Jeremiah 29:11, God says, "For I know the thoughts that I think toward you … thoughts of peace and not of evil, to give you a future and a hope."

After Saul was removed by God as king of Israel and died in battle against the Philistines, David became king (see 1 Samuel 31:1–7). David was a former shepherd who had been selected by God to be the next king many years before. God described David as a man "after His own heart" (1 Sam. 13:13), and David had a long and prosperous reign over Israel (though not without occasional setbacks because of moral failings on David's part).

After David's death, his son Solomon became the third king of Israel. Solomon built the first temple, according to God's instructions, and it took 100,000 talents of gold (approximately 2.6 billion dollars in today's currency) and 1 million talents of silver (about 2 billion dollars in today's money) (see 1 Chronicles 29:1–19). The temple contained the Most Holy Place, where God's presence was made known to His people. The Most Holy Place was a perfect cube, thirty feet wide, thirty feet long, and thirty feet high (see 2 Chronicles 3:8).

Unfortunately, as Solomon neared the end of his life, he began to turn away from the one true God (see 1 Kings 11:4–5). This would begin the cycle of disobedience, punishment, repentance, and blessing that would accompany the reigns of the rest of the kings of Israel as they obeyed or disobeyed God. As the leader of the nation went, so did the people. When the king obeyed God, the people obeyed God and were blessed by Him. However, when the king disobeyed God, the people also disobeyed God, and then God would have to punish the king and the people. When the king repented (or a new king repented) and the people acknowledged their sin, then God would bless the people. This is why it is so important for a nation to have godly leaders. The nation must allow God to direct these leaders' paths, or the results can be disastrous.

The Fall of Israel and Judah

In 1 Kings 11:27–39, the prophet Ahijah told a man named Jeroboam that God was going to divide Solomon's kingdom and make him the ruler of ten of the tribes. When Solomon died and his son Rehoboam became king of Israel, he foolishly tried to place a heavy tax burden on the people. The people rebelled, and just as God had said, Jeroboam was made ruler over the ten northern tribes of Israel. Only the tribe of Judah remained loyal to Rehoboam (see 1 Kings 12:13–20.)

The cycle of disobedience, punishment, repentance, and blessing continued. Throughout this period of the kings, many prophets attempted to warn the people of their sin and compel them to return to God before it was too late. Finally, in 722 B.C., the Assyrians invaded and defeated the northern kingdom. The people of the northern kingdom were scattered into several different lands, never to return. Some refer to this group as "the lost tribes of Israel," but they are not lost to God, because God does not lose one thing. God knows exactly where these tribes are located, and He will call 12,000 from each tribe at some time in the future to spread the good news of God's plan of salvation. Only God knows the time when He will call these witnesses, who will make up 144,000 people from the twelve tribes of Israel (see Revelation 7:4–8).

The Babylonians defeated the southern kingdom of Judah around 586 B.C. and took the people into captivity. This period, known as the "Babylonian captivity," ended in 538 B.C. with the fall of Babylon to the Persian king Cyrus the Great, who allowed the Jews to return to Jerusalem. Later, under the leadership of men such as Ezra and Nehemiah, the exiles begin to repair the city and rebuild the temple (see Ezra 1; Nehemiah 2). The last recorded prophet to speak to the people was Malachi, who ended his short book with a prophecy that the Sun of Righteousness was coming (see Malachi 4:2).

From around 435 B.C., when Malachi penned his final words, to the birth of Jesus, the Bible is silent. Other historical books, such as those in a collection known as the Apocrypha, provide us with information about those years between the last of the captivity until the birth of Jesus.

In 330 B.C., Alexander the Great led his Greek armies to a decisive victory over the Persian Empire. After his death in 323 B.C., his empire was divided among his generals, and Ptolemy of Egypt became the ruler of Palestine. Under the reign of the Ptolemies, the Hebrew Scriptures were translated into Greek (a version known as the Septuagint, from which many of the quotations in the New Testament are derived).

In 203 B.C., Antiochus the Great came into power in Syria and captured Jerusalem from the Egyptians. His son Antiochus Epiphanes became a violent persecutor of the Jewish people, going so far as to depose the high priest in Jerusalem and sell the office to a man named Jason, who was not of the priestly line. When Antiochus went off to fight Egypt in 171 B.C., the Jews, led by Judas Maccabeus, rose up in revolt and overthrew their Syrian rulers. The Maccabees were able to shake off foreign dominion until 63 B.C., when the Roman general Pompey was invited into Jerusalem to fend off a Syrian attack. Pompey took the city from Syria, setting up the events we see unfolding in the New Testament.

The Old Testament covers the period of the Law and prophecy. In the New Testament, the books of Matthew, Mark, Luke, and John tell us of the fulfillment of the Law in the person of Jesus Christ. The book of Acts and the Epistles tell us about the evangelistic effort started by Jesus continuing today, in the period of God's grace (sometimes called *the church age*), in which we now live. The book of Revelation describes what God will do at the end of this period of grace and on into eternity.

The Birth of the State of Israel

For approximately 2,700 years, the Israelites were scattered among the nations of the world. During this time, they did not have a land to call their own. They were persecuted in many countries of the world. During World War II, Adolf Hitler tried to abolish the Jewish race, killing approximately six million Jews in the Nazi death camps. In these same death camps, Hitler had approximately seven million Christians killed.

On May 15, 1948, the British Mandate over Palestine ended, and the state of Israel was born. This event was unique in all of history: a people group who did not have a land of their own for that long a period of time had never come back and formed a nation. I believe it will not be long before Israel will build a temple and reestablish the temple worship as it existed in the days of Solomon.

Just as the nation of Israel overcame tremendous odds in conquering the land of Canaan during the time of Joshua, so also the country has had to overcome tremendous odds in its efforts to keep hold of its land today. During the Six-Day War of 1967, Israel was attacked by a coalition of Arab states that banded together to put an end to Israel's sovereignty. The Israelite army was greatly outnumbered and did not have the planes, tanks, and other military support equipment the Arab nations had. In fact, during this war, the Israel Air Force was flying the French-built Mirage, while the Arab states were flying Russian-built Migs. The Arab nations had five planes for every one of Israel's.

One would think that with such overwhelming odds the Arab states would have won without even working up a sweat. From every perspective, it appeared that the Arab nations represented the superior force, and they would decisively defeat Israel. But that was not what happened. In just one raid, the Israelites destroyed fifty-eight Arab planes and damaged ten others. By June 10, 1967, Israel had seized the Gaza Strip, Sinai Peninsula, the West Bank of the Jordan River, and the Golan Heights. Israel's territory grew three times in size, and approximately one million Arabs were placed under Israel's direct control.

On October 6, 1973, a coalition of Arab states conducted a surprise attack against Israel on Yom Kippur, the holiest day in Judaism. The odds were overwhelmingly stacked in favor of the Arab states, and it again looked as if Israel would be defeated. At the time of the attack, Israel had a little more than 3,000 soldiers protecting the Sinai Peninsula. These soldiers were met by an Egyptian army of more than 100,000 soldiers—a ratio of thirty Egyptian solders to every one of Israel's soldiers. Meanwhile, in the north, the Syrian forces attacked the Golan Heights and initially made some gains into the land. Yet God intervened, and Israel began to gain back the land that had been lost. By October 26, the war was over, and Israel had won.

Only God could have turned these events around in such a way to so greatly favor Israel. God had come to the aid of Israel and defeated its enemies. God is still in the business of performing miracles for countries and individuals. God's sovereign will cannot be changed by man.

Wars and Rumors of Wars

Today, we see Israel continuing to struggle to find peace and keep its land. Jesus told us that in the last days there would be wars and rumors of wars (see Matthew 24:6). We can see that this is the situation in the world today. Arab countries currently occupy one hundred times the land occupied by Israel, and the combined Arab population is fifty times the population of the Jews. Yet the Arabs want the little bit of land occupied by the Jewish people. The land occupied by the Jews does not contain any known oil or resources, so why do they want it? And what about the future? What lies ahead for the nations of the world and the people who live in it? It seems that the world is looking for peace in all the wrong places. True peace can only be found in God.

Down through the years, God has proven that He never lies and never forgets His promises. God is always faithful to fulfill what He says He will do. God told Abraham that He would bless all nations through his descendents (see Genesis 12:3). That blessing of all nations was fulfilled through Jesus Christ, a descendent of Abraham. God blesses all nations and individuals through His one and only Son, Jesus Christ, who takes our sins away if we trust Him to do so.

Chapter 8

The Savior Comes

When Adam and Eve disobeyed God in the Garden of Eden, the relationship between humankind and God was broken. No matter how hard Adam and Eve tried or what they did, they could not restore the fellowship with God. So God developed a plan whereby all human beings could be restored into relationship with Him. This plan, which He established before the creation of the world (see 1 Peter 1:20), was for His only begotten Son to come to earth as a human being; live a perfect, sinless life; and then die in place of sinful human beings on the cross of Calvary. When Jesus died on the cross, He paid the debt penalty of sin for every human being. This is a debt every person owes but cannot pay.

In order to restore the relationship with God, the Law under the old covenant demanded that a person live a perfect life. However, no human being, except Jesus, has ever been able to lead a perfect life. Everyone is extremely important to God, so He, in His grace and lovingkindness, made a way for Jesus to pay the price of humankind's sin so the relationship could be restored. John 3:16–17 states, "For God so loved the world that He gave His only begotten Son, that whoever believes in Him should not perish but have everlasting life. For God did not send His Son into the world to condemn the world, but that the world through Him might be saved."

The Perfect Sacrifice

Jesus was born of the virgin Mary. When He came into the world, He was fully human and fully God. This is difficult, if not impossible, for us to understand, but we know that with God, all things are possible (see Matthew 19:26).

John the Baptist, Jesus' second cousin (see Luke 1:36), was born a few months before Jesus. God sent John into the world to pave the way for Jesus. When Jesus was ready to begin His ministry, He came to John the Baptist at the Jordan River to be baptized. At this time, God confirmed to the people that Jesus was His Son with a voice from heaven that said, "This is My beloved Son, in whom I am well pleased" (Matt. 3:17; see also Mark 1:11; Luke 3:21–22).

Shortly after Jesus was baptized, He went into the wilderness, where Satan tempted Him to try to get Him to disobey God (see Matthew 4:1–12; Luke 4:1–13). From the beginning, Satan has tried—and will continue to try—to destroy God's purposes and plans for peoples' lives. He tempts and deceives human beings so they will sin and not get to heaven. Yet Satan cannot prevail against God, and his punishment. The Lake of fire is awaiting all those who follow Satan (see Revelation 20:7–10). Jesus withstood all the temptations of Satan and remained faithful and obedient to God, making Him the perfect God-man to die for all the sins of the world.

In Romans 3:23, Paul wrote that all of us have disobeyed (sinned against) God and are thus not worthy to get into heaven and live where God lives. In Romans 6:23, Paul stated that "the wages of sin is death." This means if we do not trust Jesus as our Savior, we cannot get to heaven. We will spend all of eternity in hell. The only way for us to have a chance at life in heaven was for one human being to live a perfect life and pay the penalty for our sins. This is what Jesus did for us.

After Jesus' temptation in the wilderness, He spent three years teaching the people, ministering to others, training His twelve disciples, healing the sick, performing miracles, casting out demons, and pronouncing the coming of the kingdom of God.

Toward the end of His ministry, one of His disciples, Judas Iscariot, plotted against Him with the Jewish religious leaders and arranged to have Him arrested. Jesus appeared before the religious leaders and other Jewish and Roman officials, and eventually, Pontius Pilate, the Roman governor of Judea, conceded to having Him crucified. Jesus was nailed to the cross of Calvary, and there He died for the sins of the world (see Matthew 26–27).

But that was not the end of the story. After Jesus was dead in the tomb for three days, He overcame the forces of death and rose again. After His resurrection, He appeared to His disciples, and more than five hundred other people saw Him (see Luke 24:36–49; 1 Corinthians 15:6). He remained on the earth for forty days and then ascended into heaven (see Acts 1:3–9), where He is now seated at the right hand of the Father (see Acts 2:33).

The Ultimate Choice

Through Jesus, God fulfilled His plan of salvation for all humankind. He came down from heaven in the form of a human being named Jesus, lived a perfect life, took our sins upon Himself, died on the cross of Calvary, and then rose from the dead. In this way, He restored the relationship between humankind and Him and provided a way for people to live eternally with Him in heaven.

The natural question people ask when they hear that God offers this plan of salvation is, "Saved from What?" To answer this question, we must return to the events that occurred in heaven before God created humankind. As you will recall, Satan and one-third of the created angels disobeyed (sinned against) God, which led to a war in heaven and these angels being cast out. As a result of their disobedience, Satan and his followers will spend eternity in hell. God wants to save human beings from this same destination—an eternity in hell that was reserved for Satan and his followers (see 1 Timothy 2:3–4).

Now, although God provided the means for every human being from Adam onward to escape hell, He ultimately leaves the choice up to each individual. Every human, after he or she dies, will spend eternity in either heaven or hell. Hell is a lake of fire, and those who are cast into it will be tormented day and night for eternity. Heaven, on the other hand, is a perfect and beautiful place, and those who go to heaven will live in perfect peace and harmony with God for all eternity. Each one of us has to make this ultimate choice about where we will spend eternity: heaven or hell.

So how does one get to hell? One gets to hell by doing *nothing*. If a person fails to receive the forgiveness of sins from Jesus Christ by trusting Him as Savior, that person will spend eternity in hell. Each person has to make his or her *own* decision about where to spend eternity—no one can make this decision for someone else.

How does one get to heaven? Those who get to heaven will do so by placing their faith in Jesus as their personal Savior and Lord. There is no other way to get to the Father (see John 14:6). This is simply by faith—nothing more, nothing less, and nothing else. As the apostle Peter proclaimed to the religious leaders, "[Jesus] is the 'stone which was rejected by you builders, which has become the chief cornerstone.' Nor is there salvation in any other, for there is no other name [but Jesus] under heaven given among men by which we must be saved" (Acts 4:11–12). In Acts 2:21, Peter also stated, "… whoever calls on the name of the LORD [Jesus] shall be saved."

Making the Decision to Follow Christ

The cross of Calvary symbolizes God's incredible love for each one of us. It is extremely important for us to make the choice to trust Jesus as our Savior today, because there is no guarantee of how much time we have left to live. Paul wrote in 2 Corinthians 6:2, "Now is the accepted time; behold, now is the day of salvation."

If you are ready to accept Jesus as your Savior, here are the basic steps you can follow to have peace with God and spend eternity with Him in heaven:

1. Acknowledge and believe that you are a sinner in God's sight.
2. Believe that God sent His only Son, Jesus, to live a perfect life and to die on the cross of Calvary to pay the debt for your sins.

3. Confess Jesus as your Savior and Lord by asking Jesus to save you, forgive your sins, and come live within your heart and life. It is not what you do but whom you trust that saves you from an eternity in hell.

The first two steps are to *acknowledge and believe you are a sinner* and *believe that God sent Jesus to pay the debt for your sins.* The following scriptures demonstrate how all of us are sinners and in need of God's perfect sacrifice to save us from the penalty of our sins. Read each passage in the order given below. (For your convenience, these verses are also listed in appendix A.)

	Verse	**Synopsis**
1.	John 3:16	God loves everyone in the world.
2.	Romans 3:23	All people have sinned.
3.	Romans 6:23	The wages of sin is death.
4.	Romans 5:8–10	All people can be saved from hell.
5.	Acts 3:19	We must repent of our sins.
6.	Ephesians 2:8	We are saved by God's grace.
7.	Romans 10:9–13	We must confess our sins.
8.	2 Corinthians 6:2	God acknowledges our faith.

The final step is to *confess Jesus as your Savior and Lord by asking Him to forgive your sins and come live within your heart.* If you have read the above verses and are ready to receive God's free gift of eternal life, you need to call on Him in prayer. You may pray your own prayer, or if you need help in praying, you can use the following prayer and make it your own confession.

> *Lord Jesus, I know I am a sinner and in need of Your forgiveness. I know You died on the cross of Calvary to pay my sin debt for me. I now turn from my sins and ask You to forgive me. I invite You into my heart and life. I trust You as my Savior and choose to follow You as my Lord. Thank You for saving me from an eternity in hell. I ask all of this in the name of my Savior and Lord, Jesus Christ. Amen.*

Did you ask Jesus to forgive you of your sins? Did you ask Him to save you? Did you give Jesus complete control of your life? If so, welcome to God's family! Paul wrote in Romans 10:13, "Whoever calls on the name of the LORD shall be saved." Now would be a good time to pause for a moment in prayer and thank Jesus for saving you!

The Results of the Decision

Choosing to accept Christ into your life is the most important decision you will ever make. In *Our Daily Bread*, Vernon C. Grounds provided the following example of just how much of an impact it can have on a person's life:

> What a night for the Minnesota Twins baseball team in 1987! They had just defeated the Detroit Tigers and won the American League pennant for the first time in 22 years. More than 50,000 people, young and old, crowded into the Metrodome to welcome their victors home from Detroit. Banners were waving, horns were blaring, the crowd was cheering. There were even tears of joy. The players were surrounded by members of the news media. One reporter in the crowd called out to Greg Gagne, the Twins' star shortstop, and commented, "This has got to be the greatest moment of your life." Quietly Gagne replied, "Actually, no. That was the moment I asked Jesus Christ into my life."[1]

If you accepted Jesus as your Savior, you have become a joint heir with Jesus Christ (see Romans 8:17), and your name has been permanently placed in the Lamb's Book of Life (see Revelation 21:27). The Lamb's Book of Life is God's list of all the people who make the decision to trust in Jesus as their Savior.

Now that you have trusted in Jesus as your personal Savior, the next step is to grow in your Christian life by reading God's Word, the Bible, and worshiping God. God accepts you as you are, right where you are, but He never expects you to just stay there. He wants you to grow and mature in your relationship with Him so you can become all He wants you to be. For this reason, you need to seek out a Bible-believing and Bible-teaching church, where you can worship God and study His

Word. (To help you find a new church home, appendix B contains a list of the characteristics a Bible-believing church will possess.)

In Genesis 3:9, when God asked Adam and Eve the soul-searching question, "Where are you?" He knew exactly where Adam and Eve were—both physically and spiritually. What He wanted to know was whether Adam and Eve wanted to grow spiritually so that they could serve Him better or they wanted to shrink back and not serve Him, as they had been doing. Today, God is asking each one of us the same question. Will we shrink back and lose God's blessings, or will we grow and receive them?

For those who have accepted Jesus as their Savior, life on this earth will be the worst they will have to endure. However, for those who never accept Jesus as their Savior, life on this earth will be the best they will ever know. In other words, the best is yet to come for the saved person, while the worst is yet to come for the person who never trusts in Christ. Psalm 34:15 tells us that God always watches over those who follow Him and that He hears the cries of those who call out to Him.

Your new life in Christ begins the day you accept Jesus as your personal Savior, and it never has an end. God will be with you each and every day, no matter what circumstances come your way, and you can rest in the assurance that when this life is over, you will experience eternity in heaven with God. Hebrews 13:5–6 states, "For He [God] Himself has said, 'I will never leave you nor forsake you.' So we may boldly say: 'The LORD is my helper; I will not fear. What can man do to me?'"

May God richly bless you as you begin your new life.

Chapter 9

The Church Age

When Jesus completed His work on Calvary, it fulfilled a prophecy made by the prophet Daniel more than 400 years before (see Daniel 9). When Jesus rose from the grave, He completed the plan of salvation, which is a gift from God. Daniel also prophesied about another time period after Jesus rose from the grave, but no time was given as to when that period would start or end. That is the period we are in today, and it is known as the church age.

The people who followed God prior to the time when Jesus completed His work on the cross of Calvary looked forward to the day when Jesus would pay their sin debt, and they were saved by their faith (see John 8:56–58; Romans 4:1–2). Those of us who live in the time after Jesus completed His work on the cross look back on what Jesus has done, and we are saved by our faith in Him.

Prior to the time of Jesus' death on the cross, the Holy Spirit did not live within each believer's heart. Instead, the Holy Spirit lived within the hearts of individuals whom God called for a specific purpose. Once the specific purpose was completed, the Holy Spirit would depart from that individual. When Jesus ascended into heaven to take His place at the right hand of God, He sent the Holy Spirit down from heaven to live within each believer's heart. This event occurred fifty days after Jesus ascended into heaven, on the Day of Pentecost.

When Jesus was departing from the earth, He told the disciples, "But you shall receive power when the Holy Spirit has come upon you; and you shall be witnesses to Me in Jerusalem, and in all Judea and Samaria, and to the end of the earth" (Acts 1:8). After He was taken away, the disciples returned to Jerusalem and went into an upstairs room to wait for the fulfillment of the promise. The believers at that time numbered about 120 individuals (see Acts 1:9–15).

On the Day of Pentecost, a sound like the rushing of a mighty wind filled the house, and what appeared to be tongues of fire sat on each of them. They were filled with the Holy Spirit and began to speak with other tongues (see Acts 2:1–4).

Starting in Jerusalem and going to many parts of the then-known world, the apostles began to spread the good news of how one gets to heaven. Their efforts were met with strong opposition from all fronts. Some of the apostles were beaten in public, taken to court, put in jail, told never to preach again, ridiculed, and treated as scum for telling the people how to get to heaven. In spite of the persecution, the apostles established many churches throughout the world. Today the message of how one gets to heaven is being spread all over the world in many different languages.

Now, when a person accepts Jesus as Savior, the Holy Spirit comes and lives within that individual permanently. When God looks on the heart of a person who has accepted His Son, Jesus, as Savior, He sees the Holy Spirit and counts that person as righteous (because the Holy Spirit is righteous, not because the person is righteous). However, when God looks on the heart of a person who has not trusted in Jesus as Savior, He does not see the Holy Spirit and therefore considers that person unrighteous.

The period of grace that began when Jesus completed His work at Calvary will continue until God takes His people to heaven. This event is known as the rapture of the church. In 1 Thessalonians 4:13–17, Paul described this event as follows:

> I do not want you to be ignorant, brethren, concerning those who have fallen asleep, lest you sorrow as others who have no hope. For if we believe that Jesus died and rose again, even so God will bring with Him those who sleep in Jesus. For this we say to you by the word of the Lord, that we who are alive and remain until the coming of the Lord will by no means precede those who are asleep. For the Lord Himself will descend from heaven with a shout, with the voice of an archangel, and with the trumpet of God. And the dead in Christ will rise first. Then we who are alive and remain shall be caught up together with them in the clouds to meet the Lord in the air. And thus we shall always be with the Lord.

The church, or body of Christ, is made up of all those who have trusted in Jesus as their Savior. When the rapture takes place, Jesus will take all of those in the church to live with Him in heaven. There, they will be joined by those who already died after putting their faith in Jesus. No one knows when the rapture will take place; there are no prophecies that need to be fulfilled before Jesus can return and take the born-again believers with Him to heaven. Only God knows when the rapture will occur, so it is important for us to live as though it will happen at any time. For those who have accepted Christ, worshiping God is not an option; it is mandatory. Worship is something we *want* to do because we love Jesus.

In Daniel 12:4, God told the prophet, "But you, Daniel, shut up the words, and seal the book until the time of the end; many shall run to and fro, and knowledge shall increase." This increase in knowledge can be seen today—technology is advancing at such a rapid pace that a personal computer bought today will be obsolete within two to three years. Because of signs such as these, many people have tried to predict when Jesus will come to take His church to heaven, and some have even gone so far as to set dates. For example, in 1988, Edgar C. Whisenant, Jr. published his book *On Borrowed Time,* in which he gave eighty-eight reasons why the rapture would occur on September 11, 12, or 13, 1988. Of course, these dates came and went, and God did not come to take those who have trusted in Jesus to heaven. No one has ever been able to accurately predict when Jesus will come, and no one ever will be able to do so. However, even though we do not know *when* the church age will end, we can be certain that it *will* end and that God *will* take His people to heaven.

God is giving us this time so people can make a decision as to whether or not they want to live in a perfect place called *heaven* to serve and worship Him. God does not and will not force Himself on anyone; nor will He force anyone to accept Jesus as Savior. The choice is up to each individual to make. Once a person trusts Jesus as Savior, a relationship and fellowship is established with God. The relationship can never be broken, but the fellowship can be broken by sin, and that sin must be dealt with before the fellowship can be restored. For this reason, when we sin, we must tell God of our sin, stop the act of sinning, and ask God to forgive us in order to restore the fellowship (see 1 John 1:5–10).

Chapter 10

The Tribulation

When Jesus was sitting with His disciples on the Mount of Olives, they asked Him, "What will be the sign of Your [second] coming, and of the end of the [church] age?" (Matt. 24:3). Jesus replied by describing a series of signs that would precede His second coming to earth. These signs will be fulfilled in a seven-year tribulation period that will come after the end of the period of grace, and it will begin immediately after the rapture of the church. Note that the rapture is thus not the second coming of Jesus, because Jesus will not come to earth for the second time until after this tribulation period has occurred.

Often people wonder why hurricanes, tornados, earthquakes, mudslides, tsunamis, terrorist attacks, and other disasters and evil things happen. These terrible events are happening everywhere today, but they are nothing compared to what will take place during the seven years of tribulation that are yet to come.

In 2 Chronicles 15:2, God tells us why this period of tribulation with all of its terrible events is going to happen: "The Lord is with you while you are with Him. If you seek Him, He will be found by you; but if you forsake Him, He will forsake you." When individuals or nations forsake God, He will forsake them. The United States of America was founded upon people's faith in God, and its laws are based on the Bible. Yet today, many people in the United States have forsaken God and want to remove all traces of Him from this country. If we do away with everything relating to God and everything that is based on God's Word, the United States of America will become a lawless nation. It will be like the Old West—we will no longer have any laws, and the person who is the fastest draw and most-accurate shooter will win every time. Is this the kind of country we want our children, grandchildren, and other loved ones to grow up in? Or do we want our country to return to God?

If people in our nation continue to forsake God, we can expect this great country to go the way of other great world powers that rejected Him. Empires such as Egypt, Greece, Rome, Assyria, and Babylon once ruled the entire known world, but these nations are mere shades of what they once were. In Galatians 6:7–8, Paul wrote, "Do not be deceived, God is not mocked; for whatever a man [person] sows, that he will also reap. For he who sows to his flesh will of the flesh reap corruption, but he who sows to the Spirit [God] will of the Spirit [God] reap everlasting life." A person always reaps what he sows.

The Trumpet Call

One day in the future, God's archangel will sound a trumpet call, and all those who have trusted in Jesus as their Savior will ascend into heaven. The dead who trusted in Jesus will rise first, and then those who are alive will rise and meet Jesus in the air (see 1 Thessalonians 4:15–18). As mentioned in the last chapter, we do not know when this event, called *the rapture,* will take place. However, according to the prophet Daniel, we know that the tribulation period will start immediately after the rapture and that it will last for seven years:

> Seventy weeks are determined for your people and for your holy city, to finish the transgression, to make an end of sins, to make reconciliation for iniquity, to bring in everlasting righteousness, to seal up vision and prophecy, and to anoint the Most Holy. Know therefore and understand, that from the going forth of the command to restore and build

> Jerusalem until Messiah the Prince, there shall be seven weeks and sixty-two weeks; the street shall be built again, and the wall, even in troublesome times. And after the sixty-two weeks Messiah shall be cut off, but not for Himself; and the people of the prince who is to come shall destroy the city and the sanctuary. The end of it shall be with a flood, and till the end of the war desolations are determined. Then he shall confirm a covenant with many for one week; but in the middle of the week he shall bring an end to sacrifice and offering. And on the wing of abominations shall be one who makes desolate, even until the consummation, which is determined, is poured out on the desolate.
>
> —Daniel 9:24–27

When the word *week* is used in the book of Daniel, it represents seven years. (Each "day" represents one year.) This means that those who remain on earth after the rapture will not have the Holy Spirit dwelling within them; only those who have trusted Jesus as their Savior will be taken to heaven. Although Satan does not know when the tribulation period will begin; he just knows he will have seven years after the rapture to do his work on earth before the battle of Armageddon begins. Satan has to have his Antichrist ready to come forward at any time, with short notice. This Antichrist will take over the rule of the world because there will be no Christians to oppose him.

The Seals

During the tribulation, God will pour out His wrath on the nations and individuals of the world. In the book of Revelation, these judgments are depicted as seven seals on a scroll (see Revelation 5:1). The judgments will begin during the first half of the tribulation period and continue to the end of the seven years. As the seals are broken, the following will take place:

1. First seal: When the first seal is broken, a rider on a white horse will come forth. He carries a bow and has a crown (see Revelation 6:2; Daniel 9:24–27). This represents the time when the Antichrist will sign a peace treaty with many nations,

ushering in a short, unprecedented period of peace in the world. The entire earth will be under the rule of the Antichrist.

2. Second seal: When the second seal is broken, a rider on a red horse will go out, and the entire world will break out in war (see Revelation 6:3–4). This account parallels Daniel 8:24, which speaks of a time of assassinations, wholesale killings, revolts, massacres, and other horrible things that have never before been seen on such a large scale.
3. Third seal: When the third seal is opened, a rider on a black horse will come forth, causing a worldwide food shortage. Famine will be rampant throughout the earth, and nations will have to ration food and water (see Revelation 6:5–6). We have seen famine and starvation in the past, but it will be as nothing compared to what will occur during the tribulation period.
4. Fourth seal: After the rider on the black horse is sent out, the fourth seal will be broken, and a rider on a pale horse will emerge. The rider's name is Death, and he is followed by Hades. Wars, famine, plagues, and wild beasts will then kill one-fourth of the global population (see Revelation 6:7–8).
5. Fifth seal: When the fifth seal is broken, God will avenge the souls of the believers who were martyred on earth during the tribulation (see Revelation 6:9–11).
6. Sixth seal: After the sixth seal is broken, God will use His power to cause great disturbances in the universe. There will be great earthquakes. The moon will become red like blood. The sun will turn black, and the stars will drop to earth like a fig tree drops its late figs (see Revelation 6:12–17). It is possible that global warming could be setting the stage for this future event. The sixth-seal judgment ends exactly three-and-one-half years after the start of the tribulation period.
7. Seventh seal: There appears to be a pause between the sixth- and seventh-seal judgments. This may well be to allow the people living in the world at this time to reconsider their choice to follow God or Satan. The choice can only be one or the other; either a person will choose to spend eternity in heaven with God or in hell with Satan.

The seventh seal contains the seven trumpets and the seven bowl judgments. These judgments of God are so incredible that all of heaven is silent for thirty minutes (see Revelation 8:1).

The First Half of the Tribulation

When Israel and its leaders rejected Jesus as the Messiah during His entry into Jerusalem just a few days prior to His crucifixion, God designated the Gentiles to spread the gospel during the church age. Yet God will give the Israelites another chance during the tribulation period. At the time of the rapture, God will return the spiritual world on earth to the way it was before Jesus came, and He will give the Holy Spirit to those whom He calls to do His work on earth. Once each called person has completed the task God wanted him or her to complete, the Holy Spirit will leave that person. God will not send the Holy Spirit to live within individuals who trust Jesus as their Savior during this time as He does today.

God will provide two witnesses to bring His chosen people (Israel) back to Him. There is much speculation as to the identity of these two witnesses, but many believe they will be Moses and Elijah. In Matthew 17:10–11 we read, "His disciples asked Him [Jesus], saying, 'Why then do the scribes say that Elijah must come first?' Jesus answered and said to them, 'Indeed Elijah is coming first and will restore all things.'" It is also interesting to note that when Jesus took Peter, James, and John to the top of the Mount of Transfiguration, the disciples recognized Moses and Elijah; although, they had never seen them or been introduced to them. From this, we know God will provide a means for His people, the Jews, to recognize Moses and Elijah when the time comes.

For the first half of the tribulation period (three-and-one-half years), these two witnesses will teach the Israelites about God, just as they did in the Old Testament. There will be 144,000 Israelites who trust Jesus as their Savior during this short time (see Revelation 7:4–8).

Immediately after the rapture, the Antichrist will begin to identify his followers by giving them a special identification called *the mark of the beast.* Many people will believe they will be able to get into heaven by not taking the mark of the beast. However, this is not the case, because simply refusing to take the mark does not equal trusting in Jesus. The people who pass from the church age into the tribulation will have a great delusion come upon them so that those who already have heard the Word of God and understand how to get into heaven will not accept Jesus (see 2 Thessalonians 2:9–11).

During this time, God will select 12,000 Israelites from each of the twelve tribes of Israel and will seal and protect them so Satan cannot keep them from witnessing for God (see Revelation 7:1–8). It is not known how God will seal these witnesses or what He will use to seal them, but some theologians believe it will be with the Holy Spirit. These 144,000 Israelites will be witnessing for God, and they will be witnessing to both the Israelites and the Gentiles (those who entered the tribulation and have never heard the Word of God). These will be the people who will have a chance to accept Jesus as their Savior. Every person who gets to heaven will get there in exactly the same way as everyone else: by placing his or her trust in Jesus.

The Israelites will also restore temple worship similar to what was practiced during the reign of King Solomon. This means the temple must be rebuilt and the practice of animal sacrifices reinstituted with the priesthood in place. Depending on how one counts the number of temples built in the past, this would be the third temple. The first temple, built by Solomon around 960 B.C., was destroyed by the Babylonians around 587 B.C. The second temple, built by Herod the Great around 19 B.C., was destroyed by the Romans in A.D. 70. It was this second temple Jesus visited and in which He taught the people.

The Jewish people are in the process of collecting money and other needed furniture for this third temple. They already have one hundred pounds of gold put aside for the golden candlesticks that will be used in the rebuilt temple. Using today's prices for gold—$600 per ounce—this means that the Jewish people already have approximately $960,000 in place with which to rebuild the temple.

Currently, the Muslims have a place of worship called the Dome of the Rock that sits on the ancient grounds where the temple once stood in Jerusalem (though not on the exact location of Solomon's temple). As we noted in a previous chapter, Abraham is the father of both the Israelite and the Muslim races, so this creates a real problem. Shortly after Isaac was born, Sarah saw the son of Hagar the Egyptian scoffing, and she told Abraham to cast out Hagar, this bondwoman, and her son (see Genesis 21:8–14). The Angel of the Lord told Hagar, Ishmael's mother, that he would be against every man and every man would be against him (see Genesis 16:7–12). Periodically, tensions erupt between Muslims and Jews over the site, as occurred in 1996 during the "Tunnel Riots," when Israeli antiquity authorities began excavating beneath the Temple Mount. Given the current political state of affairs surrounding the site, it is unclear how the Israelites will be able to build a temple in Jerusalem. However, God will work it out.

During this time, the Antichrist will rise to power and begin to solve the problems of the Middle East. He will somehow enable the Israelites to build a new temple and restore temple worship with its animal sacrifices. This will be quite a feat, as many talented political leaders over the years have attempted to solve the problems of the Middle East with no success.

It is possible that the Antichrist could come from a revived ancient Roman Empire and be empowered by Satan. In Daniel 11:37–38, the prophet wrote, "He [the Antichrist] shall regard neither the God of his fathers nor the desire of women, nor regard any god; for he shall exalt himself above them all. But in their place he shall honor a god of fortresses; and a god which his fathers did not know he shall honor with gold and silver, with precious stones and pleasant things." One interpretation of this scripture is that Satan's Antichrist will be homosexual and that he will place his faith in his military strength to win any war.

We read in Daniel 9:27, "Then he [the Antichrist] shall confirm a covenant with many for one week [seven years]; but in the middle of the week [seven years] he [the Antichrist] shall bring an end to the sacrifice and offering." This shows that the Antichrist will make a peace treaty among nations for seven years, but after three-and-one-half years, he will break this treaty.

The Last Half of the Tribulation

At this point, Satan will lead his angels against God, and there will be another war in heaven. God will win the war, and Satan and his angels will be cast down to the earth (see Revelation 12:7–9). Satan can read the Bible as well as we can, so he knows when this occurs, he will have just three-and-one-half years before he is locked up in the bottomless pit for 1,000 years. Satan will know his time is short, so he will intensify the persecution of Israel (the woman who gave birth to Jesus that is recorded in Revelation 12:13). During the tribulation period, Satan will also persecute the people who trust Jesus as their Savior (see Revelation 12:17).

Satan will come and sit in the Holy of Holies in the temple of the Israelites. He will claim to be God and will deceive many (see Revelation 13:1–15). Satan has always strived to be God, but he cannot and will not take God's place. God gives each of us a choice: choose God or Satan. If we choose God, our eternal destiny is heaven; if we choose Satan, our eternal destiny is hell and torment. Satan's arrival in the temple of the Israelites will signal the start of the seventh seal judgment and the last half of the tribulation period.

The first three-and-one-half years of the tribulation will be a terrible time of judgment, but it will pale in comparison to the events that will occur during the second half of the tribulation. When the seventh seal is broken, seven angels who stand before God will be given seven trumpets (see Revelation 8:2). As each angel sounds his trumpet, a judgment will take place on the earth. These trumpet judgments are as follows:

1. First trumpet: the angel of God destroys one-third of the trees and all of the green grass on the earth (see Revelation 8:7).
2. Second trumpet: the angel destroys one-third of the sea life and a third of all ships (see Revelation 8:8–9).
3. Third trumpet: the angel destroys one-third of the fresh water in the rivers and springs, leaving less water for the people of the earth to drink (see Revelation 8:10–11).
4. Fourth trumpet: This angel destroys one-third of the sun, moon, and stars. This might represent how many angels fell with Satan (see Revelation 8:12–13).
5. Fifth trumpet: The next three trumpet judgments represent three woes that will befall the earth, with each woe being much

worse than the previous one. When the fifth angel sounds his trumpet, he unleashes judgment that torments, but does not kill, every person on earth for five months. This judgment will not affect the 144,000 Jewish witnesses God sealed or their converts, those who have decided to trust Jesus as their Savior (see Revelation 9:1–12).

6. Sixth trumpet: This angel will free four of Satan's angels, who will kill one-third of the entire world's population (see Revelation 9:13–21). This is the second woe.
7. Seventh trumpet: There is another pause between the sixth trumpet and the seventh trumpet judgments (see Revelation 10:1–11:14). When the seventh angel sounds his trumpet, seven angels are given bowls with which to pour out more judgments. This is the third and final woe.

While these seven judgments are being unleashed on the earth, Satan will require anyone who wishes to purchase goods and do business to receive the mark of the beast (see Revelation 13:16–17). Many people will accept the mark just to survive. No one knows what this mark of the beast will be, but some have speculated that it will be the number 666, which is the numerical value of the name of the Antichrist (see Revelation 13:18). (Each letter of the Greek and Hebrew language has a numerical value assigned to it; for example, the name of Jesus in Greek has a value of 888.)

Several years ago, it was believed that the mark of the beast was the social security numbers assigned to citizens of the United States of America. However, the mark of the beast must be unique worldwide; and while social security numbers are unique in the United States, there is no assurance they will be unique in the entire world. The mark could well be a microchip implanted under the skin, similar to what veterinarians use today for identifying pets.

Since the attacks of September 11, 2001, there has been growing pressure in nearly every part of the world to give each person a unique identification number. The mark of the beast could thus be a credit card with a digitized picture, fingerprint, eye scan, DNA code, or other means of identification. With such a system in place, all Satan would have to do with people who want to conduct commerce is swipe the assigned identification card. If it matches Satan's records, the person would be allowed to buy or sell; if not, the person would be arrested and dealt with according to the laws in force at that time.

When the seventh angel sounds his trumpet, the seven bowl judgments will begin. These judgments will ultimately usher in the events that will lead up to the establishment of 1,000 years of true peace on the earth, called *the millennium*. During this time, Jesus and those who have trusted Him as their Savior will rule (Rev. 11:15–19). The seven bowl judgments are as follows:

1. First bowl: when God's angel pours out the first bowl judgment, it will cause foul and loathsome sores to come upon the people who follow Satan (see Revelation 16:2).
2. Second bowl: this angel will pour out the second bowl on the sea, which will turn to blood and cause all living things in the sea to die (see Revelation 16:3).
3. Third bowl: This angel will pour his bowl on the freshwater rivers and springs. The third trumpet judgment already destroyed one-third of the fresh water supply on earth, and this third bowl judgment will now turn the remaining fresh water into blood. All living things in the water will die, and there will be no fresh water for the people to drink (see Revelation 16:4–7). It is interesting to note that people can live only a few days without water.
4. Fourth bowl: the fourth angel will pour his bowl on the sun, causing it to scorch the people with fire (see Revelation 16:8–9).
5. Fifth bowl: The fifth bowl will be poured out on the throne, or capital city, of Satan, and the entire world will be filled with darkness. At this point, the people will be trying everything to get relief from the pain of the sores, the lack of water, and the scorching flames, but nothing they do will alleviate their suffering (see Revelation 16:10–11). They will want to die but will be unable to do so. This is a preview of what is to come for them in hell.

6. Sixth bowl: God's sixth angel will pour out his bowl on the Euphrates River, causing its waters to dry up. This judgment will cause the whole world to gather its military forces together to do battle with God. This will be known as the battle of Armageddon, during which God will defeat Satan and his followers (see Revelation 16:12–16).
7. Seventh bowl: God's seventh angel will pour out his bowl into the air. When this bowl is poured out, God will speak from the temple of heaven and say, "It is done!" The earth will experience an earthquake greater in force than any earthquake that has ever taken place in all of history. Great hail will fall upon the people, some of which will weigh approximately seventy pounds (see Revelation 16:17–21).

After God has poured out His wrath on the nations and individuals of the world, the stage will be set for the last battle and the end of the tribulation period: the battle of Armageddon.

The Battle of Armageddon

In Joel 3:12–14, the prophet said this battle will take place in "the valley of decision." This valley, also known as the Valley of Armageddon and the Valley of Jehoshaphat, begins in northern Israel and extends approximately 250 miles south to the city of Jerusalem. God will bring all the nations to this valley, where He will render His final judgment (see Joel 3:2).

The battle will begin when the military powers of the world mobilize to attack Israel. Although the reason for the attack is unknown, we can see some possible motives today in the Muslim extremists who vow to kill all Jews and every person allied with the Jews. The "king of the south" (Egypt and its African allies) will make a pact with the "king of the north" (Syria and its allies) to attack Israel (see Daniel 11:11). The Antichrist and his army from the west will move to preserve his kingdom, and at the same time, an army of 200,000,000 soldiers will come from the east (see Revelation 9:16). All the armies will meet in the Valley of Decision to do battle (see Daniel 11:40–45; Revelation 19:19–21).

It is at this time that the second coming of Jesus, the Messiah, will take place. Jesus will come from heaven, riding on a white horse, and will touch down on the Mount of Olives (see Matthew 24:30). This is the same place where Jesus ascended to heaven.

The battle of Armageddon will be the largest and worst battle ever fought. God will pour out His wrath on the nations and individuals of the world (see Revelation 19:14–15), and so many will be killed that the blood of the fallen will touch the horses' bridles (see Revelation 14:19–20). One-third of all humankind will perish (see Revelation 9:15).

At the conclusion of the battle, God will capture Satan and all of his angels. He will lock them up for one thousand years in the bottomless pit, and they will not be able to escape (see Revelation 20:1–2). He will put the Antichrist and the False Prophet into the lake of fire, or hell. These will be the first to go into hell (see Revelation 19:20). God will then judge the nations and individuals who have not repented of their sins and accepted Jesus as their Savior.

The three reasons God will pour out His wrath on the nations and individuals are as follows:

1. Because of what the nations and individuals have done to His people, the Israelites (see Joel 3:2).
2. Because the nations and individuals have failed to repent of their sins against God (see Revelation 16:9).
3. Because of the ways the inhabitants have abused the universe God created (see Revelation 11:18).

Jesus, the Messiah, will now enter Jerusalem through the Golden Gate. This is the same gate He entered a few days prior to His crucifixion on Calvary, when the Jewish leaders rejected Him as the Messiah. This time, the Israelites will accept Him, and God will set up His earthly kingdom.

Escaping the Wrath to Come

So, what will those who have accepted Jesus as their Savior be doing while these events are taking place? By the time the tribulation comes, all those who trusted Jesus to save them will have been taken up to heaven. They will be having a wonderful time of fellowship with God while the tribulation is being carried out on earth! The reasons why God will take His people to heaven before the tribulation period are as follows:

1. God says He does not change. "For I am the LORD, I do not change" (Mal. 3:6). "Jesus Christ is the same yesterday, today, and forever" (Heb. 13:8).
2. God is not the author of chaos. "God is not the author of confusion but of peace" (1 Cor. 14:33).
3. God makes us righteous once we put our trust in Jesus as our Savior and Lord. "For He [God] made Him [Jesus] who knew no sin to be sin for us, that we might become the righteousness of God in Him [Jesus]" (2 Cor. 5:21).
4. God is good and will not punish the righteous. "To punish the righteous is not good, nor to strike princes for their uprightness" (Prov. 17:26).
5. God says He will keep those who follow Him from the hour of trial. "Because you have kept My [God's] command to persevere, I also will keep you from the hour of trial [tribulation period] which shall come upon the whole world, to test those who dwell on the earth" (Rev. 3:10).

Oh, how thankful I am that because of the trust I have put in Jesus as my Savior, I do not have to go through the tribulation! I thank God for saving me not only from the tribulation but also from hell itself.

You too can escape the tribulation and hell by placing your trust in Jesus to save you from such terrible and awful suffering. If you have not already done so, please review the "Making the Decision to Follow Christ" section in Chapter 8 and invite Jesus into your life today.

Chapter 11

The Millennium

According to Daniel 12:11–12, there will be a gap of seventy-five days from the end of the battle of Armageddon to the beginning of the millennium. During these seventy-five days, it is believed that the third temple in Jerusalem will be cleansed according to the laws God gave to Israel in the book of Leviticus and the nations will be judged for the way they have treated the Israelites. All those who have not trusted Jesus as their Savior at the end of the tribulation period will be sent to hades, the holding place for unsaved people, to be tormented until the final judgment at God's great white throne judgment. This means that only those who are saved will enter the millennium.

God's glory will fill the earth, and He will be the absolute ruler. He will have a perfectly righteous government and give justice to everyone. After He judges the nations of the world, He will give the people a pure speech so that they can worship Him (see Zephaniah 3:9), and all the nations and people of the world will honor Him in Jerusalem and keep the Feast of Tabernacles (see Zechariah 14:16–19). Approximately one-third of the Gentiles (see Revelation 6:8; 9:15) and one-third of the Israelites (see Zechariah 13:8–9) will have survived the tribulation period. These are the ones who trusted Jesus as their Savior during that time of trial and who will live in the millennium.

For a period of 1,000 years, God and His saints will rule, and there will be peace on earth (see Daniel 7:27).These saints will be made up of two groups. The first group will consist of those who accepted Jesus before the tribulation and were taken to heaven during the rapture. The second group will consist of those people who accepted Jesus during the tribulation period and died before the millennium began. The millennium will mark the beginning of God's kingdom and will last for all eternity.

Satan and his angels will be locked up in the bottomless pit during this time (see Revelation 20:1–3), and while he is there, he will not be able to provoke individuals to hatred or persecute the people of the world. For one thousand years, Satan, the great deceiver, will be unable to deceive anyone!

As mentioned in Chapter 7, when the northern kingdom of Israel fell to the Assyrian invaders, the people were taken to many different lands and never returned. Some Bible scholars refer to these peoples as the "lost" tribes of Israel. Yet, as also mentioned, God never loses anything. Although these tribes have been scattered all over the world for thousands of years, at the beginning of the millennium, God will identify them and restore them. This will include the tribe of Levi, which served as the temple priests (see Revelation 7:4–8). God will give Israel all the land He promised Abraham and his descendants in the Old Testament (see Genesis 15:18–21; Ezekiel 47:15–21).

The nations of the world will report to the ruling saints and God, and there will be peace and justice during this period. In fact, it is hard to comprehend the perfect conditions that will exist under God's rule. There will be no wars, no rumors of wars, and no sickness. Animals will not devour each other, attack humans, or fight among themselves (see Isaiah 11:6–7; 65:25). There will be no road rage, no foul verbal language, no obscene sign language, no murders, no stealing, no immorality, no abortions, no disasters, and no crime. No one will even lose his or her temper.

God will make many changes for the betterment of the earth and its environment. The saints will administer the world for God and keep it clean and perfect (see Isaiah 65:17–25). Nothing in nature will be out of balance. The rain will come when it is needed, and there will be no floods in the land. There will be no more global warming and no more deserts, because they will blossom as a rosebush (see Isaiah 35:1–2). The Dead Sea will come alive and be filled with abundant fish (see Ezekiel 47:1–9). The earth will no longer have tainted air or water, and the environment will be free of all contaminates. Can you imagine a pure and clean earth?

Doctors and hospitals will no longer be needed, because the people living during the millennium will have no allergies, sinus conditions, heart problems, colds, flu, or other diseases such as AIDS and cancer. Food, clothing, and shelter will be available for everyone. There will be no sadness, because no one will die during this period, and there will be no reason to be sad. The food will be free of contaminates—no radiation.

Social injustices and bigotry will no longer exist. The Israelites will no longer be persecuted as they have been for centuries (see Isaiah 60:15). There will be no more terrorists, global conflicts, mobs, gangs, riots, or clashes with the police. There also will be peace in the Middle East.

Only those people on the earth who have trusted Jesus as their Savior and are alive after the battle of Armageddon will come through the tribulation period and into the earthly kingdom God will establish. It will be a healthy and safe place, where people can enjoy living and raising their children. There will be no physical death, so people will have children and live to see those children grow up to have more children, and then see those children have more children. After one thousand years, there will be many individuals born on earth who never had the chance to choose between an eternity with God in heaven or an eternity with Satan in hell. In fact, some may never have even heard of Satan or know anything about him.

God wants everyone to be saved, but He gives individuals the final decision as to whether or not they will accept that salvation. Everyone who goes to heaven gets there the exact same way as everyone else: by trusting Jesus as Savior. God desires to have only those people in heaven who have chosen to be there.

Because those who are born during the millennium will not have been given the chance to make that choice, after one thousand years, God, in His infinite wisdom, will free Satan from the bottomless pit for "a little while" (Rev. 20:3). Only God knows how long Satan will be free, but it will be for exactly as long as God needs to make sure that everyone has been given the chance to make his or her decision. Even after living in a perfect environment and being ruled by a perfect and righteous God, many will think the grass is greener on the other side and will choose Satan instead of God.

Satan will then defile the world with his disobedience and again mess it up. After being free for a while to achieve his purpose of tempting and deceiving the inhabitants of the earth, he will gather the nations together to do battle against God one last time (see Daniel 7:13–14; Revelation 20:7–10). Satan, his angels, and his allies will surround the beloved city of Jerusalem, but God will quickly defeat them all. This will be the final battle ever to be fought. Satan and his followers will then be cast into the lake of fire (hell), where the Antichrist and False Prophet are being tormented.

There is a song titled "Victory In Jesus" that has been sung in many congregations around the world. This song describes the ultimate victory that all who have put their trust in Jesus are looking to see. Remember, God made hell (the lake of fire) for Satan and the angels who followed him (see Matthew 25:41). He never intended for human beings to reject Him (even though He knew some would) and therefore join Satan and his angels in hell.

The next event to take place is the great white throne judgment. In Romans 14:11, Paul writes, "For it is written: 'As I live, says the LORD [Jesus], every knee shall bow to Me, and every tongue shall confess to God.'" Those who have trusted Jesus as their Savior have already bowed their knee and confessed to God. Their names are already written in the Lamb's Book of Life, so they will not go through the great white throne judgment. They will be tending the perfect environment and earth God set up at the beginning of the millennium (see Revelation 20:11–15).

Only those souls who rejected Jesus as their Savior will be resurrected and brought before God. These souls who appear before the great white throne are destined to spend eternity in hell. This will be the most horrible event possible for these individuals, because they will finally acknowledge that Jesus is God, bow down and worship Him, and then be cast into the lake of fire (hell) for all eternity because they did not make that choice when they had the chance.

Chapter 12

The New Heaven, New Earth, and New Jerusalem

Most people want to know why there is going to be a new heaven, a new earth, and a new Jerusalem. The reason is because when Satan is released from the bottomless pit at the end of the millennium, he will again pollute the earth, heaven, and Jerusalem with his lies and deception. God, in His infinite wisdom, will make everything new and perfect once more, and this time, Satan and his angels will not be released to corrupt it.

In Isaiah 65:17, the prophet Isaiah received word from God that this would come to pass: "For behold, I [God] create new heavens and a new earth; and the former shall not be remembered or come to mind." Likewise, in Revelation 21:2, John stated, "Now I saw a new heaven and a new earth, for the first heaven and the first earth had passed away. Also there was no more sea." There will also be a new Jerusalem.

How will the old earth be destroyed? After God wiped out all of humankind in the great flood (with the exception of Noah and his family), He made a covenant with Noah and his descendents that He would never again destroy the people of the earth with water (see Genesis 9:8–17). (When you see a beautiful rainbow in the sky, you can be reminded of this covenant God made with us.) According to 2 Peter 3:7, 10–13, the old heaven and earth will instead be destroyed with fire:

> But the heavens and the earth which are now preserved by the same word, are reserved for fire until the day of judgment and perdition of ungodly men.... But the day of the Lord will come as a thief in the night, in which the heavens will pass away with a great noise, and the elements will melt with fervent heat; both the earth and the works that are in it will be burned up. Therefore, since all these things will be dissolved, what manner of persons ought you to be in holy conduct and godliness, looking for and hastening the coming of the day of God, because of which the heavens will be dissolved, being on fire, and the elements will melt with fervent heat? Nevertheless we, according to His promise, look for new heavens and a new earth in which righteousness dwells.

Notice that the new earth will not have any seas. Our world as we know it is three-fourths water, but the new earth will have a completely different terrain. God's righteousness will dwell there, and it will be perfect in every way for all eternity. There will be no more disobeying God in the new heaven and the new earth, because God will remove the sin nature from the people who live there.

Today, Satan has access to heaven (see Job 1:6–12), but this will not be the case in the new heaven, because he will be locked up in hell for all eternity. God will remove the curse He placed on the earth when He put Adam and Eve out of the Garden of Eden (see Genesis 3:17). Sin will be no more.

In John 14:2–4, Jesus says, "In My Father's house are many mansions; if it were not so, I would have told you. I go to prepare a place for you. And if I go and prepare a place for you, I will come again and receive you to Myself; that where I am, there you may be also. And where I go you know, and the way you know." All who ultimately experience the new heaven and earth will do so because they trust in Jesus and love Him for who He is and what He did for them on the cross of Calvary.

Jesus is the one who makes it all possible. Right now, He is in heaven making a place for those of us who have put our trust in Him so that we can live eternally with Him. All too often, we fail to recognize that what God wants for us is the best for all of eternity.

Can you imagine having such a perfect place to live? The only experience many of us have with a new home is with one that was built for us on this old earth—and believe me, a new house is not even close to being perfect. The water heater in the basement may leak. The roof might not have been constructed properly and may need to be repaired. The plumbing may need work. The temperature inside may be either too hot or too cold and never the same throughout the house. There are a multitude of imperfections that can plague a new home, but the house Jesus is building for us will not have any of those flaws, and the temperature inside will be just right. In other words, it will be perfect in every way.

In addition to the new heaven and new earth, there will also be a new Jerusalem. This new Jerusalem will be the capital city of heaven, and it will be a paradise, with God as the head (see Revelation 21:9–27). The holy presence of God will always abide in the city. Remember, no human being can live in the presence of a holy God, so, once again, there will not be any humans in heaven or the new Jerusalem. Sin, or disobeying God, will no longer exist, so those who are there will live to obey God, and there will never be another war in heaven.

It is not known where the new Jerusalem will be located. Some scholars believe it will be in outer space, while others believe it will be on the earth. However, God does give us a little insight into its size. Revelation 21:16 states that the city is a perfect cube, with sides twelve thousand furlongs long. This would make the new Jerusalem approximately 1,500 miles long on each side of the cube. To put this in perspective, astronauts orbit the earth about 200 to 300 miles above it. If the new Jerusalem were to be on earth, it would extend fifteen hundred miles into outer space, making the earth lopsided. But with God, all things are possible. The bottom line is that no one knows where the new Jerusalem will be located except God.

If the new Jerusalem is fifteen hundred miles long on each side of the cube, it would mean that the volume of the cube would contain more than three billion cubic miles of space. This would be enough space to hold everyone who has ever been born, with room to spare. However, only those people who have trusted Jesus as their Savior will be in the new Jerusalem. Note also that there will be no temple in the city, for God will be the temple. There will also be no sun or moon, for God's glory will give more than enough light. Some scholars even believe the new Jerusalem will replace the sun (see Revelation 21:22–23).

The new Jerusalem will have a wall around it approximately 200 feet thick, with twelve foundations made of precious stones. It will have twelve gates, one for each of the twelve tribes of Israel, which will each be made of a single pearl (see Revelation 21:12–21). Can you even visualize a pearl that would be large enough to make a gate? The city itself will be made of pure gold (see Revelation 21:18). Transportation will not be a problem, because all residents will have new bodies that will allow them to move quickly through the universe at extremely fast rates of speed. Just think: no cars to break down, no traffic jams, no gridlock, no accidents, and no more drunk drivers.

Words cannot describe God and all of His wonderful attributes. God knows everything there is to know. He knows each and every person who has ever been born or will ever be born. No one can hide or escape from His knowledge—He knows what every person has done, is doing, or will do. God is everywhere at the same time and is so powerful that the very elements of the universe obey His command. God could simply speak and the entire universe would be destroyed. God was not created for people, but people were created by God and for God. God demands first place in each individual's life and in that person's nation as a whole. This is the time when God will be first place.

God is an awesome, living God and is worthy to be praised and worshiped. It is a privilege, a pleasure, and an honor to be one of God's children. As members of the family of God, we become joint heirs with Jesus Christ, the one who made it all possible (see Romans 8:17). The Christian life begins when we put our trust in Jesus as our Savior, but it is a life that never ends. The people who die without trusting Jesus as their Savior will never know the beginning of this Christian life or what it is like to live it. Because they never come to know Jesus as their Savior, they will spend eternity in hell.

You can choose to become a child of God and spend all eternity with Him in heaven, but the choice is ultimately up to you. As you conclude this book, if you have not made a decision to trust in Jesus, I again encourage you to refer back to Chapter 8 and review the section titled "Making the Decision to Follow Christ."

We are not made by our dreams or by the things we possess but by the choices we make. Where will you spend eternity? The choice is up to you.

APPENDIX A

SCRIPTURES TO SHOW HOW ONE GETS TO HEAVEN

The following Scripture verses, first listed in Chapter 8, demonstrate how all humans are sinners and are in need of God's forgiveness. Read each passage in the order given below.

> John 3:16: "For God so loved the world that He gave His only begotten Son, that whoever believes in Him [trusts Jesus to save him or her] should not perish but have everlasting life."
>
> Romans 3:23 (emphasis added): "For *all have sinned* and fall short of the glory of God."
>
> Romans 6:23: "For the wages [consequences] of sin is death, but the gift of God is eternal life in Christ Jesus our Lord."
>
> Romans 5:8–10: "But God demonstrates His own love toward us, in that while we were still sinners, Christ died for us. Much more then, having now been justified [made acceptable to God] by His [Jesus'] blood, we shall be saved from wrath through Him [Jesus]. For if when we were enemies we were reconciled [made acceptable] to God through the

> death of His Son, much more, having been reconciled [made acceptable], we shall be saved by His life."
>
> Acts 3:19 (emphasis added): "*Repent* therefore and be converted, that your sins may be blotted out, so that times of refreshing may come from the presence of the Lord."
>
> Ephesians 2:8: "For by grace you have been saved through faith, and that not of yourselves; it is the gift of God."
>
> Romans 10:9–13 (emphasis added): "If you *confess* with your mouth the Lord Jesus and *believe* in your heart that God has raised Him from the dead, you will be saved. For with the heart one believes unto righteousness, and with the mouth confession is made unto salvation. For the Scripture says, 'Whoever believes on Him [Jesus] will not be put to shame.' For there is no distinction between Jew and Greek, for the same Lord over all is rich to all who call upon Him. For 'whoever calls on the name of the LORD shall be saved.'"
>
> 2 Corinthians 6:2: "Behold, now is the day of salvation."

If you have read the above scriptures and are ready to receive God's free gift of eternal life in heaven after you die, *you need to call on Him in prayer*. You may pray your own prayer, or if you need help in praying, you can use the following sinner's prayer and make it your own confession.

> *Lord Jesus, I know I am a sinner and in need of Your forgiveness. I know You died on the cross of Calvary to pay my sin debt for me. I now turn from my sins and ask You to forgive me. I invite You into my heart and life. I trust You as my Savior and choose to follow You as my Lord. Thank You for saving me from an eternity in hell. I ask all of this in the name of my Savior and Lord, Jesus Christ. Amen.*

Appendix B

Characteristics of a Bible-Believing Church

There are several characteristics of a vibrant, Bible-believing church in which people who have accepted Jesus as their Savior and Lord can worship and become more like what Jesus wants them to be. Some of these characteristics are listed below.

- The pastor and the people in the church believe the Bible is God's holy Word and is true in every aspect.
- The people put nothing ahead of God.
- The people publicly acknowledge Jesus as their Savior by being baptized.
- The people believe studying the Bible, praying, and meditating on God's Word is the way to obtain spiritual growth and is pleasing to God.
- The people believe God's work is the most important work in the entire universe for individuals, groups, and nations.
- The people believe God has a plan for each person who has accepted Jesus as Savior and He will give that person a future and a hope.

- The people share the love of God with everyone, regardless of status, race, nationality, or what that person might have done in the past.
- The people believe the only way for a person to get to heaven is by trusting in Jesus—nothing more, nothing less, and nothing else.
- The people have a passion and concern for those who have not trusted in Jesus as their Savior.
- The people believe the God of the Bible is the one and only true and living God.
- The people give all thanks, praise, and worship to the one and only true and living God.
- The people believe God alone rules over the entire universe.
- The people believe God is all-powerful, all-knowing, and everywhere at the same time.
- The people believe that all people who have trusted Jesus as their Savior are members of God's family, which is headed by Jesus.
- The people believe Jesus wants each person who has accepted Him as his or her Savior to become more like Him, because that person is a joint heir with Him.
- The people understand that nothing is impossible with God.
- Finally, the people believe God is love and that we should demonstrate that love to others through our lives and actions.

APPENDIX C

SEQUENCE OF GOD'S EVENTS

Each of the major events shown on the charts on the following pages has been given a Roman numeral for identification purposes. Below is a brief description of each major event.

I. Before God Created the Universe

Before God created the universe, He created angels. The number of angels He created is unknown and is not relevant to understanding the charts. Satan was one of the created angels. Sometime after God created the angels, Satan decided he would be like God and disobeyed God (and therefore sinned). This caused a war in heaven, in which one-third of the angels followed Satan. At this point, all of the created angels made a decision to either follow God or reject God. God then put a plan together that would save all the people who trusted in Jesus as their Savior. That plan is called *the plan of salvation.*

II. God Creates the Universe

God created the universe for people to live in while they decided either to trust God or accept Satan. There are only two choices: trust God or, by either direct decision or doing nothing, accept Satan. When God created the universe, it was perfect in every way. The environment was in perfect balance—there was not too much water, there was the right amount of sunshine, the temperature was not too cold or hot but just right. Nature and all things in the universe were in perfect harmony.

III. God Creates Adam

God created Adam first and then took a rib from Adam and made Eve. God put them in the Garden of Eden to live. God had a relationship and fellowship with them until they disobeyed (sinned against) Him.

When a person trusts Jesus as his or her Savior, the relationship and fellowship are restored. Once the relationship has been restored, it can never be broken again, but disobedience or sin always breaks our fellowship with God. God wants to walk and talk with us just as He did with Adam and Eve.

IV. Adam to Noah

There are two deaths: one is a physical death in which the body dies; the other is a spiritual death in which the spirit goes to one of two places for all eternity. Before Jesus' death on the cross of Calvary, His burial, and His resurrection, a person's spirit went to either paradise or hades when he or she died. Prior to Jesus' death on the cross of Calvary, people were saved by trusting that Jesus would one day come to earth and die for their disobediences (sins). The spirits of those who trusted Jesus as their Savior went to paradise. Otherwise, the spirits went to hades.

During this period, Satan tried to destroy God's plan of salvation by having some of his fallen angels have sex with all the females—therefore forever removing the possibility of a virgin birth of Jesus. God took these evil angels that were having sex with the females and locked them up. God flooded the world with water, and all the people perished except Noah and his family.

V. Noah to Abraham

God selected Abraham to be the head of His chosen people. God's chosen people were to tell the people of the world how to get to heaven. At this time, the people spoke one language; therefore, communication was simple and straightforward.

The people of the earth decided they would build a tower to get to heaven without trusting what Jesus would do for them in the future on the cross of Calvary. God saw what the people were doing and was displeased, so, in His infinite wisdom, He scattered the people and gave them different languages.

VI. Abraham to the Cross of Calvary

God selected Abraham to be the head of His chosen people and worked with them to get them to be faithful and obedient to Him. However, this group of people, the Israelites, continued to worship idols and things other than the one and only true and living God. Eventually, the Israelites rejected God as their leader and asked for a king. They also did not evangelize the people of the world as God had intended for them to do. As a result, they were conquered by the Assyrians (722 B.C.) and the Babylonians (586 B.C.).

> Jesus, the only Son of God, was born of a virgin, came to earth, and lived a perfect sinless life. He selected His apostles, taught the people, performed miracles, and reached out to the people of Israel. However, He was rejected, falsely accused by the religious leaders of the time, abused, and crucified on the cross of Calvary by the Romans. He rose the third day and lives in heaven today. Jesus paid the sin debt we all owe but can never pay. Jesus' disciples and more than five hundred other people saw Jesus alive after He was crucified and rose from the grave.

The death, burial, and resurrection of Jesus marked the end of Daniel's 483 years of prophecy. Sometime after Jesus died on the cross of Calvary, He took the people who were living in paradise to heaven. In this way, Jesus eliminated paradise upon His death so that today the spirits of the people who have trusted Jesus to save them can go directly to heaven. The spirits of those who have not trusted Jesus still go to hades, and then, at the time of the great white throne judgment, will eventually go to hell.

VII. Church Age

The church is the body of all people who have trusted Jesus as their Savior. We are currently living in the church age, which is also known as the period of grace. At the end of the church age, all those who have trusted Jesus as their Savior will be taken to heaven in the rapture and will receive a resurrected body similar to the one Jesus had after He rose from the grave. The end of the church age will signal the beginning of the tribulation period. All of these coming events, including the end of the church age, are in the future, and no one but God knows when these events will occur.

VIII. Tribulation Period

This is the seventh week, or the last seven years, of Daniel's prophecy. During the first three-and-one-half years of the tribulation, the Antichrist will make a pact with Israel, and the world will pull together and cooperate with each other. God will begin to pour out His wrath on the nations and individuals of the world. Sometime before the middle of the tribulation period, Israel will build the third temple and reestablish temple worship.

Midway through the tribulation period, Satan will be cast down to the earth. He has always wanted to be God, so he will go into the Holy of Holies (the place where the presence of God resided in the temple during the reign of King Solomon) and declare himself to be God. The persecution of Israel will reach its greatest intensity at this point. The Antichrist will turn against Israel, and then Satan, the Antichrist, and the False Prophet will gather their armies together and surround Jerusalem.

At the end of the tribulation period, Jesus and His saints will descend from heaven, and God will defeat Satan and his armies in the battle of Armageddon. Jesus will then cast Satan and his angels into a bottomless pit for 1,000 years.

According to Daniel 12:11–12, there will be seventy-five days between the end of the tribulation period and the beginning of the millennium. During these seventy-five days, it is believed that the temple in Old Jerusalem will be cleansed according to the laws God gave Israel in Leviticus and the nations will be judged for the way they have treated the Israelites. Jesus will then set up His earthly kingdom and rule the world for 1,000 years.

IX. Millennium

Just as the name implies, this period will last for 1,000 years. Jesus Christ, the Messiah, will set up His headquarters in Jerusalem, and He and His saints will rule the world. This will be a time of perfect rule.

X. End of the Millennium

At the end of the millennium, Satan and his angels will be loosed from the bottomless pit for a short time. This will take place so the people who came through the tribulation and those who were born during the millennium will have the choice to follow God or Satan. There is no indication as to the exact duration of this period of time, but at the end of it, Satan and his angels will be cast into the lake of fire (called *hell*), where they will be tormented for all eternity. During this period, the people who reject God and accept Satan will go to hades when they die.

XI. Great White Throne Judgment

After Satan and his angels are cast into the lake of fire, those who rejected God and accepted Satan will be brought out of hades and stand before God at the great white throne judgment. The people will learn who Jesus is and what they have missed by not trusting in Jesus as their Savior. They will bow down, worship Jesus, acknowledge Him as the Savior, and then join Satan and his angels in hell.

XII. New Heaven, New Earth, and New Jerusalem

After the millennium, God will provide a new heaven, a new earth, and a new Jerusalem for all eternity. The attributes of this environment are impossible to describe, as they will be perfect, beautiful, and pleasant in every way. There will be no tears, no troubles, no sicknesses, no sins, and no needs in this new heaven and new earth; everything will be perfect. The spirits of those who trusted Jesus as their Savior will be in heaven and have the desire to be faithful and obedient to God forever. At this point, God will have completed His plan of salvation. Sin and death will be no more, and humankind will never be separated from God again. The sin nature of all humans will be removed before they enter the new earth.

Appendix III
Sequence of God's Events: Charts
Events I

1. God creates all of the angels.
2. Satan sins against God by disobeying Him.
3. There's a war in heaven between Satan and his angels and God's angels. God won the war.
4. God makes His plan of salvation to save all human people who trust Jesus as their Savior.

Heaven

Earth

Alpha

I. BEFORE GOD CREATED THE UNIVERSE

Appendix III
Sequence of God's Events: Charts
Events II

II. GOD CREATES THE UNIVERSE

Appendix III
Sequence of God's Events: Charts
Events III

Heaven

Earth

III. GOD CREATES ADAM

At physical death, the spirit of the righteous goes to paradise.

At physical death, the spirit of the unrighteous goes to hades.

God locks up evil fallen angels.

Appendix III
Sequence of God's Events: Charts
Events IV

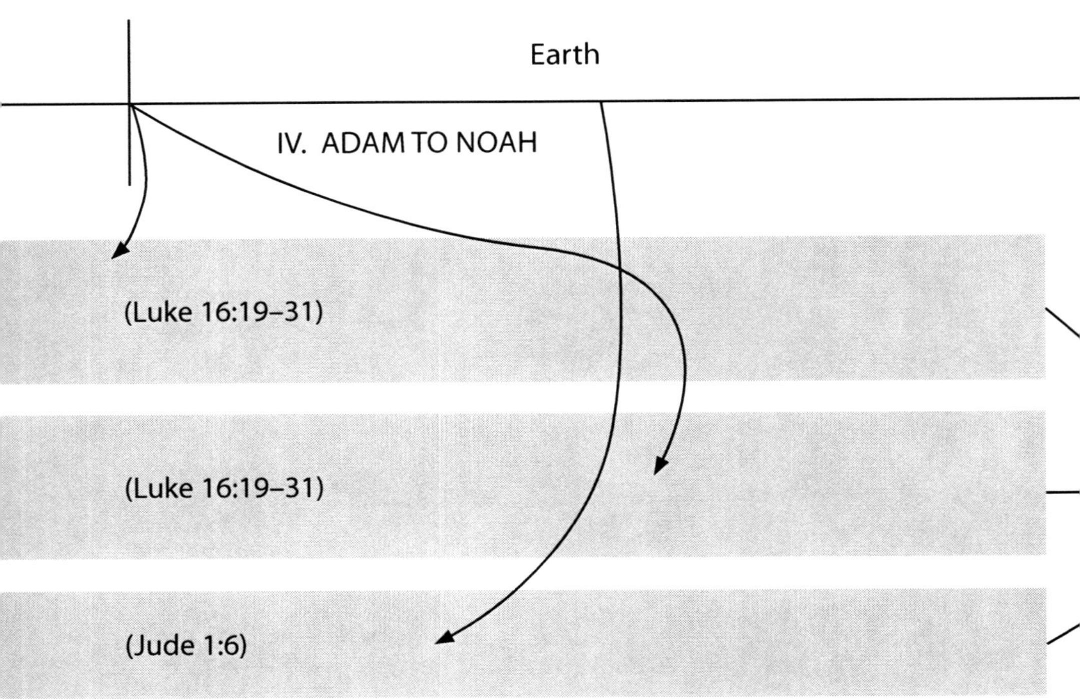

Appendix III

Sequence of God's Events: Charts

Events V

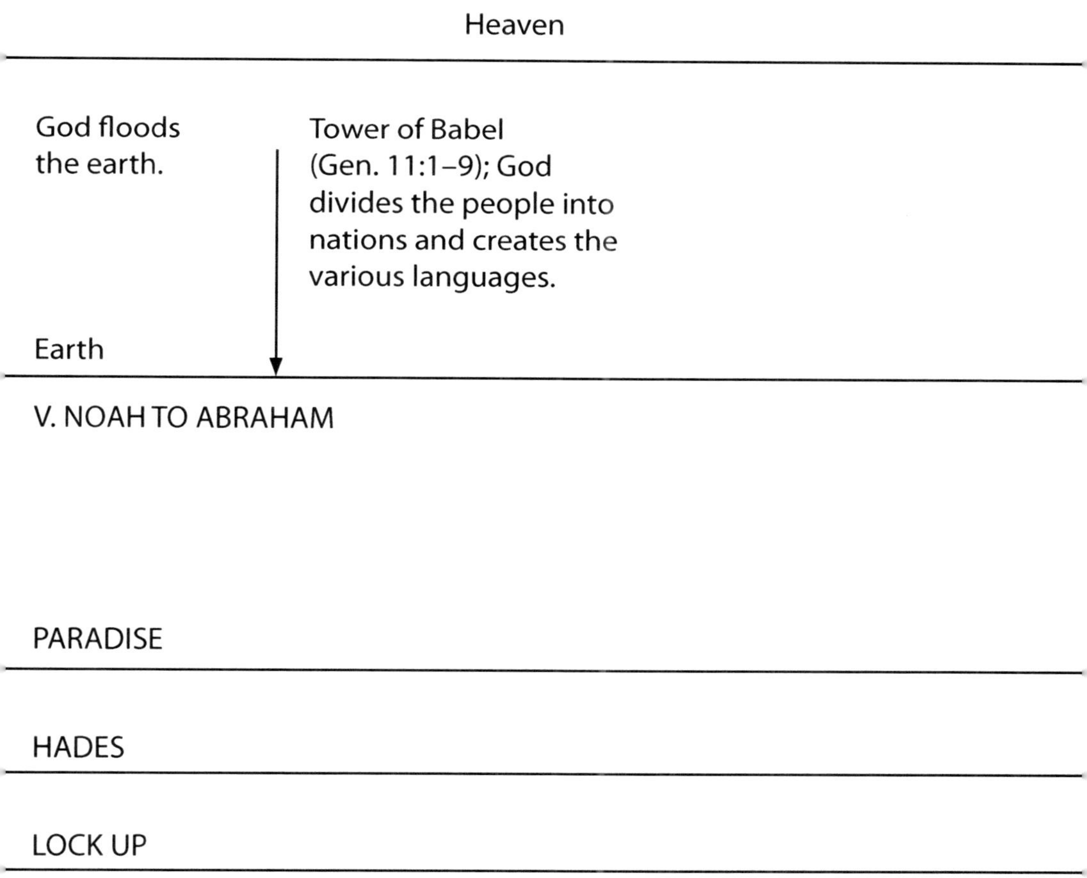

Heaven

God floods the earth.

Tower of Babel (Gen. 11:1–9); God divides the people into nations and creates the various languages.

Earth

V. NOAH TO ABRAHAM

PARADISE

HADES

LOCK UP

Appendix III
Sequence of God's Events: Charts
Events VI

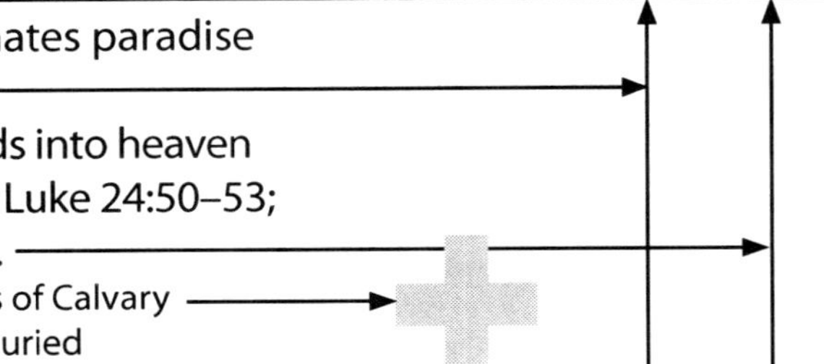

Appendix III
Sequence of God's Events: Charts
Events VII

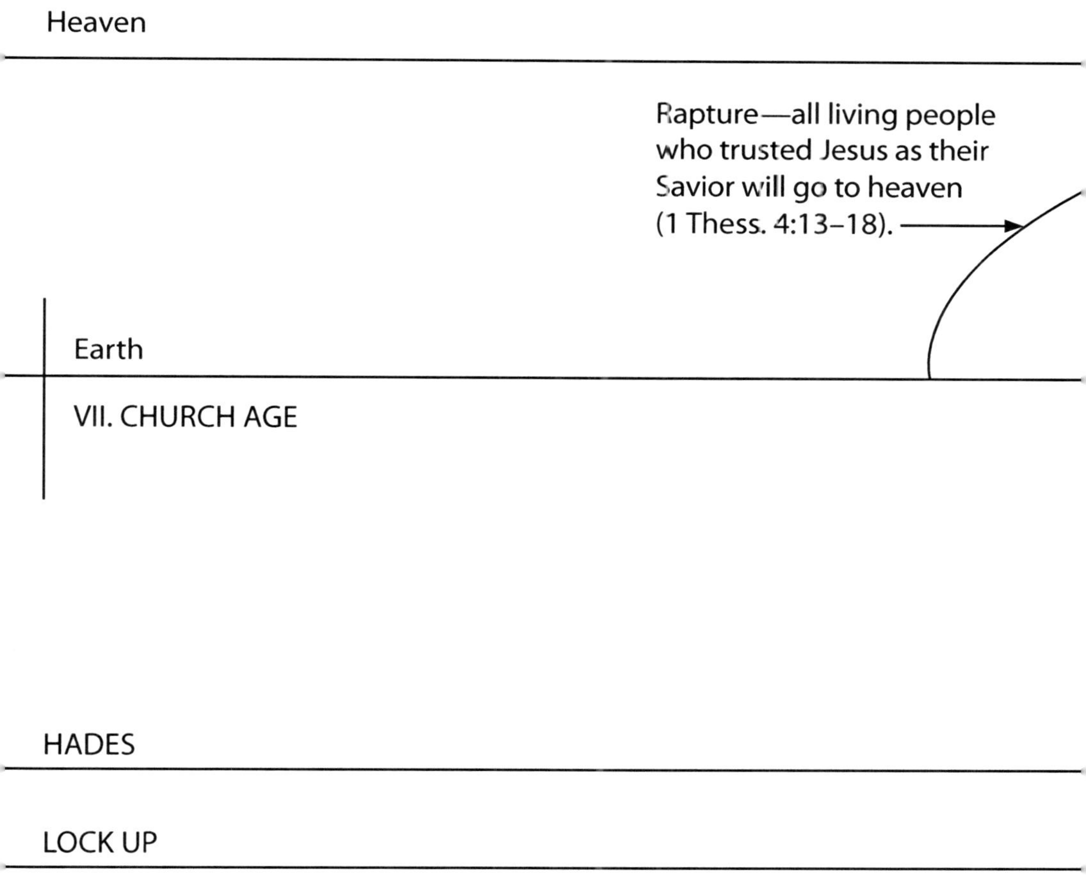

Heaven

Rapture—all living people who trusted Jesus as their Savior will go to heaven (1 Thess. 4:13–18).

Earth

VII. CHURCH AGE

HADES

LOCK UP

Appendix III
Sequence of God's Events: Charts
Events VIII

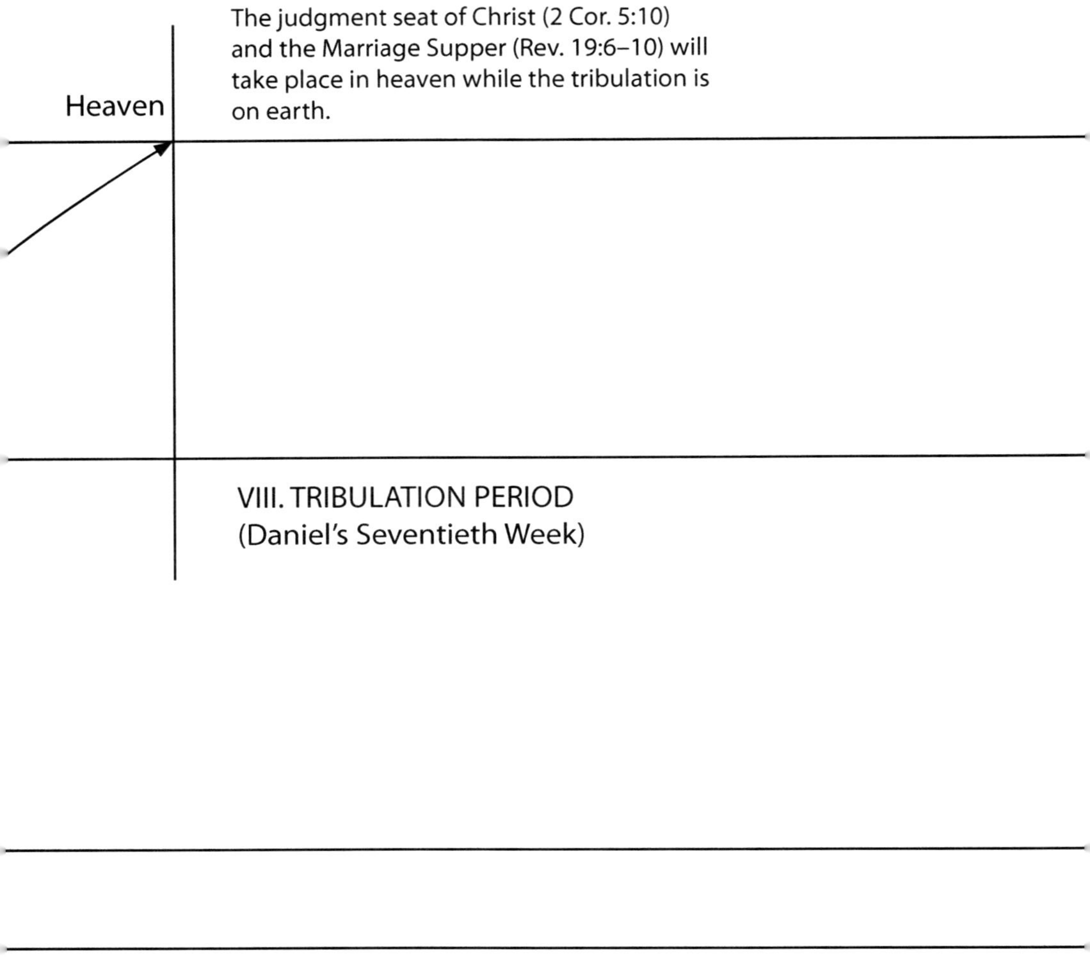

Heaven

The judgment seat of Christ (2 Cor. 5:10) and the Marriage Supper (Rev. 19:6–10) will take place in heaven while the tribulation is on earth.

VIII. TRIBULATION PERIOD
(Daniel's Seventieth Week)

Appendix III

Sequence of God's Events: Charts

Event VIII (continued)

Heaven

Earth

HADES

LOCK UP

Appendix III

Sequence of God's Events: Charts

Event VIII (continued)

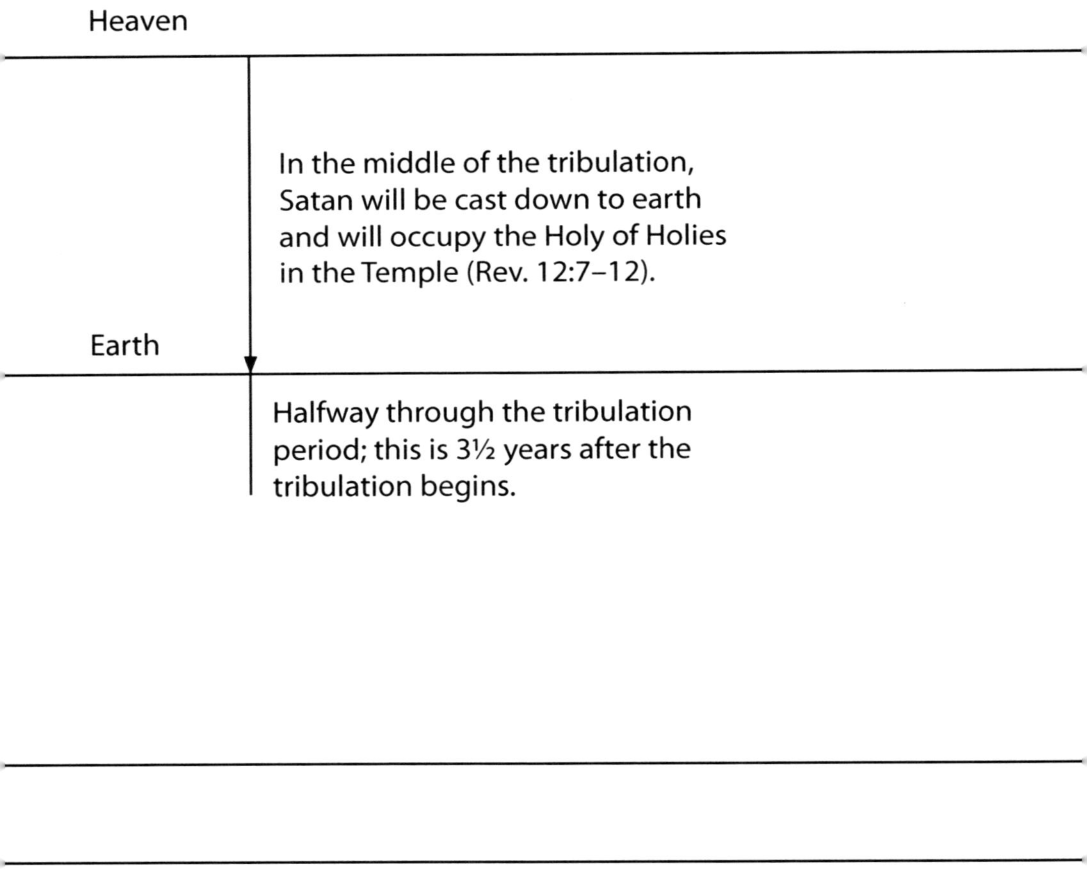
Heaven
In the middle of the tribulation, Satan will be cast down to earth and will occupy the Holy of Holies in the Temple (Rev. 12:7–12).
Earth
Halfway through the tribulation period; this is 3½ years after the tribulation begins.

Appendix III
Sequence of God's Events: Charts
Event IX and X

Jesus and His saints come down from heaven. Jesus defeats Satan and his angels (Rev. 19:11–21).

HEAVEN

The battle of Armageddon ends the tribulation period and begins the millennium.

Earth

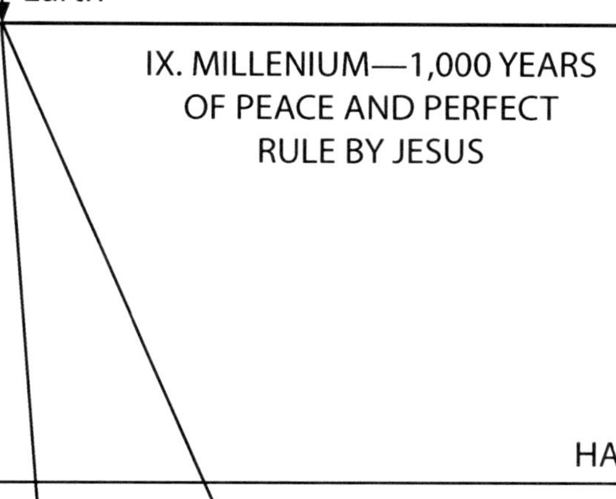

IX. MILLENIUM—1,000 YEARS OF PEACE AND PERFECT RULE BY JESUS

HADES

LOCK UP

BOTTOMLESS PIT

God locks up Satan and his angels for 1,000 years in the bottomless pit (Rev. 20:1–3).

Antichrist and False Prophet are put in hell (Rev. 19:20–21).

Appendix III
Sequence of God's Events: Charts
Event X

Appendix III
Sequence of God's Events: Charts
Event XI

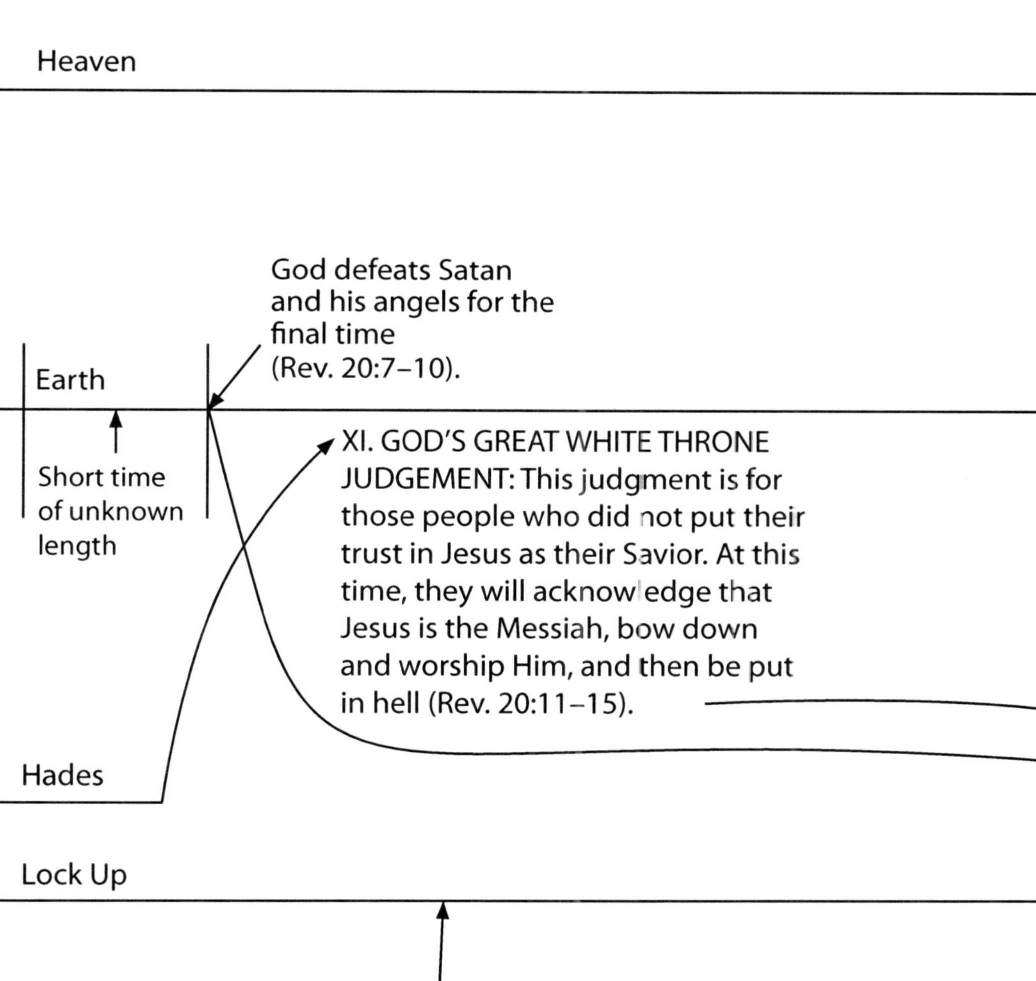

Appendix III
Sequence of God's Events: Charts
Event XII

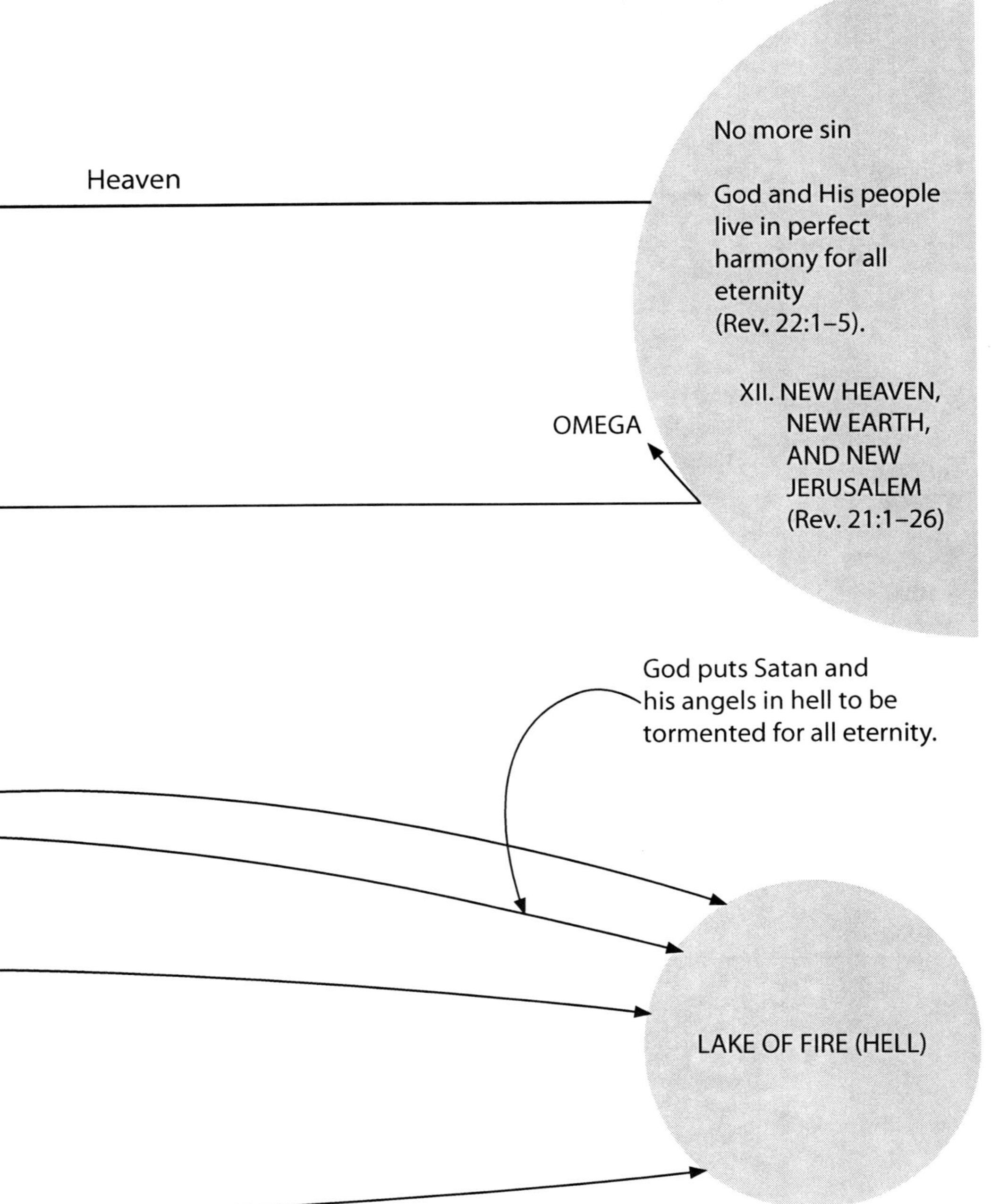

Endnotes

Chapter One

1. Peter Stoner, *Science Speaks* (Chicago: Moody Press, 1969); *Evangeline*, First Baptist Church, Jacksonville, Florida, May 23, 1971, vol. 28, no. 10.
2. Bernard Ramm, "Can I Trust My Old Testament?" *The King's Business* (February 1949), 232–233.
3. Josh McDowell, *Evidence That Demands a Verdict*, vol. 1 (Orlando, FL: Campus Crusade for Christ, 1979), 19–22.
4. John W. Montgomery, *History and Christianity* (Downers Grove, IL: InterVarsity Press, 1971), 29.
5. Ramm, "Can I Trust My Old Testament?" 232–233.
6. John W. Lea, *The Greatest Book in the World* (Philadelphia, PA: 1929), 17–18.
7. Stanley Lawrence Greenslade, ed., *Cambridge History of the Bible* (New York: Cambridge University Press, 1963), 476; Eusebius, *Ecclesiastical History*, vol. 8 (Loeb edition), II, 159, 259.
8. McDowell, *Evidence That Demands a Verdict*, 19–22.
9. Sidney Collett, *All About the Bible* (Old Tappan, NJ: Revell, 1959), 63.

10. John W. Lea, *The Greatest Book in the World,* 17–18.
11. For an in-depth analysis of the Documentary Hypothesis, see Josh McDowell, *More Evidence That Demands a Verdict* (Orlando, FL: Campus Crusade for Christ, 1975).
12. McDowell, *Evidence That Demands a Verdict*, 19–22.
13. McDowell, *More Evidence That Demands a Verdict* (Orlando, FL: Campus Crusade for Christ, 1975), 309–311.
14. Nelson Glueck, quoted in *Conversation with Dr. Earl Radmacher* (Dallas, TX: June 1972), 50.
15. Robert Dick Wilson, quoted in Davis Otis Fuller, ed., *Which Bible?* (Grand Rapids, MI: Grand Rapids International Publications, 1970), 42.
16. McDowell, *Evidence That Demands a Verdict*, 19–22.
17. For those who want an exhaustive proof that the Bible is the Word of God and true in every aspect, see the following books by Josh McDowell: *Evidence That Demands a Verdict,* vol. 1 (Orlando, FL: Campus Crusade for Christ, 1979); *Evidence That Demands a Verdict,* vol. 2 (Nashville: Thomas Nelson, 1993); and *The New Evidence That Demands a Verdict* (Nashville: Thomas Nelson, 1999).

Chapter Eight

1. Vernon C. Grounds, *Our Daily Bread* (Grand Rapids, MI: RBC Ministries, 2001). Quoted by permission.

CPSIA information can be obtained at www.ICGtesting.com
Printed in the USA
LVOW082324200612

286844LV00004B/6/P

9 781414 123820